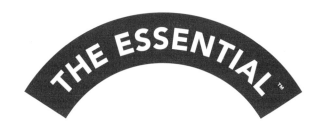

Pablo Picasso

BY INGRID SCHAFFNER

THE WONDERLAND
PRESS

Harry N. Abrams, Inc., Publishers

THE WONDERLAND PRESS

The Essential™ is a trademark
of The Wonderland Press, New York
The Essential™ series has been created by The Wonderland Press

Series Producer: John Campbell
Series Editor: Julia Moore
Project Manager: Adrienne Moucheraud
Series Design: The Wonderland Press

Library of Congress Catalog Card Number: 98-074609
ISBN 0-8362-1934-1 (Andrews McMeel)
ISBN 0-8109-5820-1 (Harry N. Abrams, Inc.)

Distributed by Andrews McMeel Publishing
Kansas City, Missouri 64111-7701

Unless caption notes otherwise, works are oil on canvas

Printed in Hong Kong

Harry N. Abrams, Inc.
100 Fifth Avenue
New York, NY 10011
www.abramsbooks.com

Contents

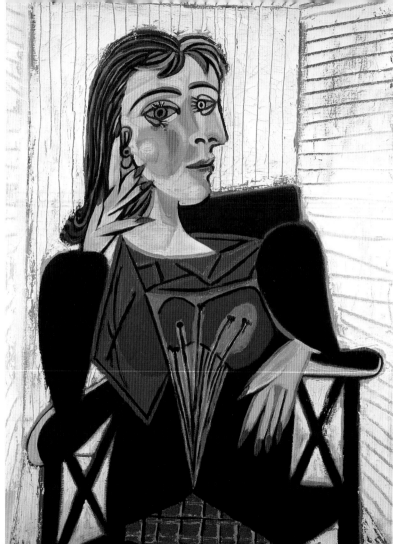

The Picasso Challenge

There is a photograph of Pablo Picasso at the peak of his career, holding a giant beach umbrella and parading down the sand behind one of his mistresses. His expression is mischievous. One reason this is such a famous image—even if you've never seen it, you can easily imagine Picasso cavorting this way—is that he practically radiates that mixture of mock seriousness and childish determination that make him such a triumphant figure of Modern art. **The original** *bad boy,* Picasso is universally seen as having influenced the course of Western art history.

The Modern Legend

From Picasso to Jackson Pollock to Andy Warhol, the stars of Modernism have often been bad boys—alienated individuals who act out against the strictures of society with a spirit of irresponsible adolescence that modern society adores. The wildly popular romance of Picasso's bad-boy reputation was minted in the images of him as:

- the successful **bohemian** in a bathing suit

- the artist as likely to be found at a **bullfight** as in his studio

- the passionate **lover** of beautiful women

5

- the proud **father** of a tribe of love children

- the creative **volcano**

- the Communist **millionaire**

- the *enfant terrible* who lived to be 91

Pablo Picasso was nothing if not publicly **hailed for his youthful antics** right up to the end of his long life. And he cultivated that legend. As a Spaniard working in France—the international headquarters of the pre-1945 art world—Picasso was an outsider who turned his marginal status into a compelling stature. He liked to see himself as a **Primitive**—a natural man living on the margins of correct society by dint of his intuitive wit and cunning within a world of his own creation. (Never mind that his art made him millions and afforded him a life of glorious luxury in Paris and in the South of France, surrounded by an élite.)

Sound Byte:

"The souls of people do not interest him.... For him, the reality of life is in the head, the face, and the body, and this is for him so important, so persistent, so complete that it is not at all necessary to think of any other thing—and the soul is another thing."

—GERTRUDE STEIN

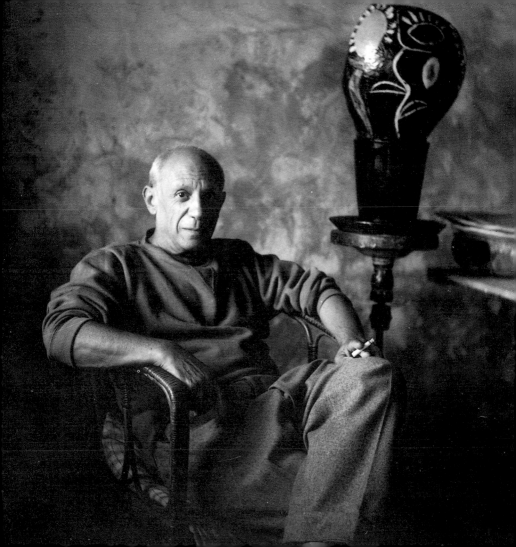

A Picasso is a Picasso is a Picasso

Now it may sound odd, but the fact that Pablo Picasso (1881–1973) is known as **the most famous artist of the 20th century** makes it all the more challenging to get to know his art. His legendary name is synonymous with creative genius and his maverick styles are instantly recognizable. No matter what period of his vast production—from his Blue- and Rose-Period pictures of harlequins, to his abstract Cubist still lifes; from his high Modernist images of women (the two-eyes-on-one-side-of-the-head sort of thing) to the masterfully tossed-off drawings of bullfights and studio allegories—you pretty much know a Picasso when you see one.

We know Picasso not only through his own **tremendous production of paintings, prints, and sculptures,** but through the endless pastiches, cartoons, wallpaper designs, arty graphics, cheesy hotel art, classy booze-bottle labels, and other spin-offs that proliferate his imagery throughout popular culture. (Indeed, Picasso is so quintessentially a 20th-century figure that to make something look "Picassoid" is as good as making it Modern.) At the same time, Picasso's Olympian achievement remains a challenge to anyone aspiring to greatness *("Like, that other guy's work was great, but he was no Picasso").* His reputation remains so huge, his art so famous that when The Museum of Modern Art in New York presented a major retrospective in 1980, the exhibition was such a hit, with such overwhelming attendance, that Pablo Picasso forever changed the meaning of the word *blockbuster*.

The Picasso Challenge

The problem with Picasso is that his reputation and fame actually interfere with his art. **We know he's great, but why?** At the end of the day, given everything you've heard about him, it's difficult to just stand in front of one of the pictures and see what it's about. The claims to greatness, the bohemian biography, the Picassoid T-shirt on the person standing next to you all clamor for attention. Ultimately, if what you're looking for is a better appreciation and understanding of the images themselves, **Picasso's fame and popularity can be distracting.** That's why you're going to love this book. It offers a solution to the Picasso Popularity Problem by going straight to the essentials of Picasso and his art. Within moments, you'll be able to answer these perplexing questions, and others:

- How (and, for heaven's sake, *why?*) did he keep changing his style?

- What role did he play in shaping the course of Modernism?

- How did his Spanish heritage affect his art?

- And what about those women?

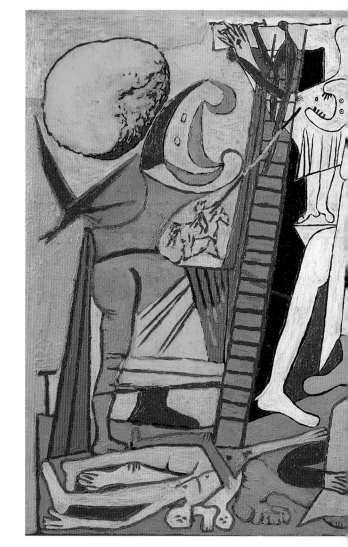

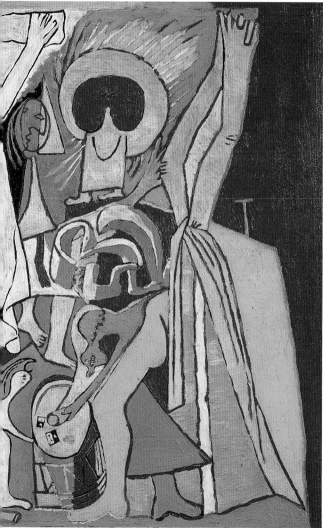

Crucifixion
1930. Oil on
plywood
20 ½ x 26 ⅜"
(51.5 x 66.5 cm)

The $48,400,000.00 Question

Let's begin with the legend. When it comes to Picasso's art, there's a special claim that critics, scholars, collectors, ticket-takers, and poodle-washers make concerning Picasso's creativity: He was… go ahead, say it… *a genius.* Almost everyone acknowledges this, even those who bash the guy for his colossal ego and silly antics. But wherein lies the greatness? This is the million-dollar question, especially if the prices paid for his art have anything to do with it. (His painting *The Dream* sold at auction in 1998 for $48,400,000.00.)

Well, Picasso's genius can be boiled down to five essential points.

GENIUS POINT NUMBER 1: THE MINOTAUR

Pablo Picasso was a *Minotaur figure.* Like the mythic creature—half-man, half-bull —with whom he identified, Picasso led a rampage through the first half of this century, starting with Cubism, but then **continually reinvented his own art,** and with it the history of Modernism.

> *FYI:* Along with **Henri Matisse** (1869–1954), the supreme colorist of Modernism, Picasso is considered the most important innovator of 20th-century art.

GENIUS POINT NUMBER 2: REINVENTION

Picasso was a prodigious talent who could change his art at will. And that's exactly what he did. His art doesn't so much *develop* as deliberately transform itself. Picasso mastered and dominated every image that inspired him, including his own art. His modus operandi was *power*. His own images continually fell subject to his power for reinvention. **No sooner did he master a style than he changed it.** No sooner did the new work begin to show signs of mannerism than Picasso moved on to an entirely new approach.

Sound Byte:
"I am not in favor of following any determined school [of painting] because that only brings about a similarity among adherents."

—PICASSO, 1897

GENIUS POINT NUMBER 3: INTROSPECTION

His art is a form of deep **pictorial self-analysis.** With every image, he's thinking:

- What can a picture *be?* (He reduces his image of a hillside town down to a painting of a bunch of cubes.)

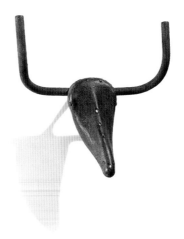

Head of a Bull
Assemblage of
bicycle saddle
and handlebars
13 ¹/₄ x 17 ¹/₈ x 7 ¹/₂"
(33.5 x 43.5 x 19 cm)

Musée Picasso, Paris.
© Photo RMN–Béatrice Hatala

- What *can be* a picture? (He picks up a pair of bicycle handles and a seat and transforms them into a sculptural representation of a bull's head simply by reassembling them.)

These were essential questions for Picasso, and he worked with the full power of his impressive will to answer and reformulate them in his art. Think of Picasso's art as *the art of thinking about art,* of taking apart the grammar of art's visual vocabulary and putting it back together in a new way.

GENIUS POINT NUMBER 4: WORK

Never satisfied, **he labored ceaselessly** at his art. His work represents a constant expenditure of energy, of working intensity. He thought of himself as a laborer in his studio, working hard every day—physically—to give form to his thinking. When he wasn't in his studio, he was doodling on a napkin or in some other way tinkering with his thoughts.

GENIUS POINT NUMBER 5 (SAVING THE ESSENTIAL GENIUS POINT FOR LAST): ART

The art itself is the ultimate testament to Picasso's legendary genius: paintings, sculptures, prints, drawings, ceramics, costumes. **Picasso turned everything he touched into vivid, compelling imagery.** A famous series of photographs shows him polishing off a trout at lunchtime, a quick pat to the pet dachshund, then voilà, he transforms the fishbones into a ceramic picture. All in the moments after a meal when the rest of us would be suppressing a burp and maybe considering dessert.

So, the Mystery is: There *is* No Mystery

Picasso's genius is simply that he worked hard—and endlessly—to express his enormous talents and rigorous visual thinking about essential questions of representation, a process that led him to constantly reinvent his own art.

> **FYI:** Though Picasso could draw like an old master by the age of 20, he claimed he spent his lifetime learning to draw like a child.

Picasso the Modern Artist

In terms of art history, Pablo Picasso is considered a **Modernist**. This is a sweeping label used during the 20th century to *declare a break from the previous century* and from historicism in general. ("History is bunk," declared modern industrialist Henry Ford.) Instead, Modernists were determined to be representative of the present, the here and now—socially, politically, culturally, psychologically. **James Joyce** (1882–1941) was a Modernist in literature; **Igor Stravinsky** (1882–1971) was one in music. In art there has been a constant stream of movements within Modernism: Fauvism, Cubism, Surrealism, Abstract Expressionism, Post-Modernism, and lots of other *-isms* in between. Picasso's art influenced all of them. His legacy continues, even if only as the subject of homage or critique, as is the case with the intriguing cosmic dialogue that Pop artist **Jasper Johns** (b. 1930) has carried on with Picasso for decades.

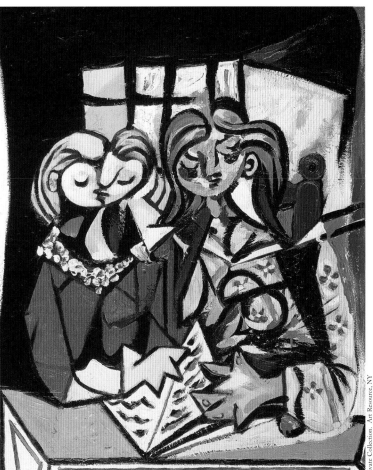

Two Girls Reading

Quintessential Modernist

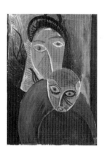

Mother and Child
1907
31 $^7/_8$ x 23 $^5/_8$"
(81 x 60 cm)

Picasso is the quintessential Modernist in that **his art is about exploring and reinventing pictorial processes.** His career cannot be seen in terms of the established tradition of an artist who masters one form of expression (say, Impressionism) and then reiterates that expression for the rest of his or her life. Instead, Picasso's work unfolds as a full platter of possibilities. He explores the prospect of depicting a group of women in one particular way and this leads to an entirely new form of representation. Along the way, each new elaboration reflects its own set of questions, decisions, problems, and resolutions. That also happens to be the official line on Modernism (and why Modernist art history is typically constructed as one *-ism* after another). Modern art is about:

- artists working out a **succession of formal possibilities** and problems.

- **pictures that reveal themselves as pictures:** Whether it's an assortment of little cubes, the color red, or a masklike expression, Modern art makes it easy to identify the pictorial elements involved in making an image.

- the *reality* **of pictorial objects:** Modern sculptures and paintings aren't mirrors of nature, but real objects in their own right.

That's why Picasso is the complete Modernist. **He never stops thinking about the nature of art as a process,** the pleasures and challenges of picture-*making,* or about finding and articulating new possibilities. So how do these possibilities unfold in his art?

Flashes & Caricatures

On the one hand, Picasso experiences a series of revelations throughout his career—think of them as *flashes!* of inspiration—which he transforms into **urgent cultural expressions.** Seeing African sculpture for the first time and meeting the painter **Georges Braque** (1882–1963) are two significant *flashes!* that result in *Les Demoiselles d'Avignon* and Cubism, respectively. On the other, he also has an incredible gift for caricature, for making a quick study of a face, an art movement, an emotion, or an experience, then stripping away the details in order to amplify aspects that convey the essence of the matter. Seeing how far he can go with his abstractions and still maintain a sense of the reality of a woman's glance, or of a dove, or of lust and joy, is one of the challenges of Picasso's art. *It's what keeps him interested in being inside his own head.*

Imagine This!

A perfect example of Picasso's power as an imagist is *Guernica* (see pages 98–100 for more details). One of the most famous antifascist statements of the century, this painting of a village massacre does not come from any direct experience of the Spanish Republicans' tragic fight for freedom. (Although he is a passionate nationalist, the Spaniard Picasso spends the war years living comfortably in French châteaux.) The mural shrieks of pain and emotion because of Picasso's genius in imagining it.

> **FYI: Photography**—Picasso maintained a vast picture archive in his studio. Recent scholarship shows that he worked extensively from photographs.

So what about those Women?

For Picasso, the metaphors of artistic creativity and reproduction intersected in one of the primary (and primal) images in his art: **women.** Since in real life Picasso was a macho man, living with a succession of women whom he immortalized in his art, there has been a tendency to anchor his images of women to their biographical interest. *(No doubt he was peeved with Dora Maar the day he painted her like that!)* But such a linking of Picasso's artistic style to the "woman of the moment" trivializes the complexity—pictorial, symbolic, psychological—of Picasso's art. (It also pays short shrift to the women themselves. One mistress's experience is referred to as *Surviving Picasso.*) On the other hand, **Picasso's women aren't just forms.** His art is full of buoyant, dreamy, maternal, and earthy women who affirm the joys of life, who offer blissful abandon, and who promise rejuvenation, sexual fulfillment, and creative nourishment. These images teem with crazed, weeping, predatory, and terribly remote women who embody Picasso's fears of sexual contact (the responsibility of children, or worse, a fatal venereal disease), his wariness of the demands of others, or of becoming alienated from his work. Collectively, Picasso's images of women—as **muses and monsters**—can be seen as the artist's attempts to dominate and distort a battery of fears and desires that express his own conflicted feelings toward life itself.

> **FYI:** Picasso was known to be a highly superstitious man who lived in fear of his own death.

Boy Wonder: Peaceful Doves and Raging Bulls

So the story begins: **Pablo Ruiz y Picasso** is born on October 25, 1881 in Málaga, in the Andalusian region of southern Spain, the son of **Don José Ruiz y Blasco** and of **María Picasso y López.** (Spanish surnames are often a combination of both parents' family names.) Don José, an academic painter of flowers and birds (especially doves, or pigeons, which are a common sight near the Picasso home), recognizes and encourages his son's prodigal talent. Legend has it that Picasso

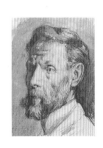

Portrait of the Artist's Father, Don José Ruiz Blasco. 1896 Watercolor 10 ⅛ x 7" (25.5 x 17.8 cm)

Museo Picasso, Barcelona. Giraudon/Art Resource, NY

FACT SHEET: HIS MISTRESSES AND WIVES

Here are the important women in Picasso's life and the years he spends with them.

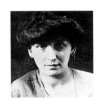

1905–11: Fernande Olivier Her book *Picasso and Friends* (1933) is a wonderful account of their life together in the bohemian "Bateau-Lavoir."

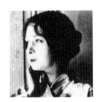

1911–15: Marcelle (Eva) Humbert He nicknames her "Eva" (as in, his ideal woman) and tattooes her name onto his Cubist pictures. Their affair ends when she dies of tuberculosis in 1915.

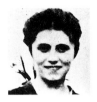

1917–35: Olga Kholkhlova A Russian ballerina with the Ballets Russes when they meet, she marries Picasso in 1918. Their son **Paulo** is born in 1921. Olga inducts Picasso into a world of classy refinements and high society, which he later rejects. The marriage ends in divorce.

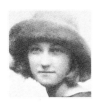

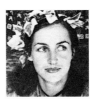

1927–36: Marie-Thérèse Walter Only 17 when they accidentally meet outside a department store and Picasso asks to paint her face. She creates for Picasso a haven of domestic bliss while he is still married to Olga; at first, he visits Marie-Thérèse in secret, then begins seeing her regularly on weekends. She is the mother of **Maïa** (b. 1935).

1936–44: Dora Maar A Surrealist artist and photographer in her own right, her years with Picasso are the subject of her 1993 memoir, *Picasso and Me*. She is featured in Picasso's painting *Weeping Woman* (see page 91). This photo of her was taken by Man Ray.

1944–53: Françoise Gilot A young painter when they meet, she is the mother of their son **Claude** (b. 1947) and daughter **Paloma** (b.1949). Her book *Life with Picasso* (1964) was the subject of the Merchant-Ivory film, *Surviving Picasso*.

1953–73: Jacqueline Roche When they meet, she's a recent divorcée; they marry eight years later, in 1961. She becomes his companion and nurse, then keeper of his flame, until her own death from suicide after discovering that she is unable to survive life without Picasso.

could draw before he could walk and that his first words were "Piz, piz!" (for "lápiz," or pencil). Judging from his early pictures of bullfights and doves, **his "career" begins by age 8.** Not only are the drawings remarkable for a child, they are thematically and personally significant. As an icon of peace and hope, the dove becomes a staple image in Pablo's own art, harking back to his childhood with all the sweetness and innocence that bird implies. On the other end of the symbolic spectrum is **the bullfight,** that dark theater of cruelty that is uniquely Spanish and to which the boy Picasso is introduced by his father. As an image of national identity and brute force, the beast becomes an alter ego for Picasso himself.

Barcelona, Baby!

In 1891, Don José accepts a teaching position in the northwest town of La Coruña, a rainy, miserable spot that he instantly dislikes, but to which he takes his wife, son, and Pablo's two younger sisters, **Lola** and **Concepción (Conchita);** the latter dies of diphtheria soon after their arrival. Pablo enjoys La Coruña, since he is able to practice drawing at the school where Don José teaches. Four years later, Don José is offered a post in Barcelona at the prestigious School of Fine Arts—also known as La Lonja—and eagerly moves his family there, in part because he wants Pablo to attend the fine academy in the capital city of Catalonia.

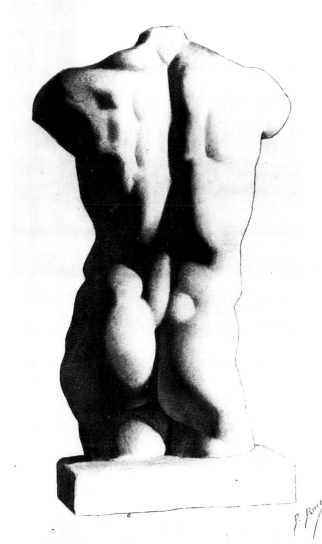

Study of a Torso,
after a plaster cast
1894–95
Charcoal on paper
19 ³/₈ x 12 ³/₈"
(49 x 31.5 cm)

Musée Picasso, Paris

Spanish Legacy

In the late 1890s, Barcelona rocks. It is a high-energy hybrid of Catalan nationalism, Basque individualism, and Parisian sophistication. En route to their vacation in Málaga in the summer of 1895, the family stops in Madrid so that Don José can show his son the Spanish national art museum, the **Prado.** There, father acquaints son with some of the Spanish masters whose ranks he will one day join:

- **Francisco de Goya** (1746–1828), whose powerfully dark vision is expressed in scathing caricatures of the aristocracy and of religious hypocrisy, as well as in scenes depicting the horrors of war (think *Guernica*);

- **El Greco** (1541–1614), the Greek mannerist who reveals his supremely spiritual vision through an idiosyncratic style of attenuated drawing (his figures look like stretched spooks) and a palette of chilly blues and silvery grays (think Picasso's "Blue period");

- **Diego Velázquez** (1599–1660), court painter to Philip IV, expresses a sumptuously aristocratic vision through intense humanism. His most famous painting, *Las Meninas* (a portrait of the princess with her maids of honor), dares to insert the artist's own self-portrait by way of a strategically placed mirror (think Picasso's *majestic ego*).

Once they arrive at their new home in Barcelona, the young Picasso astounds everyone at La Lonja with his spectacular entrance-exam submissions. He completes the exam in one day and is admitted, then proceeds to blast through what the school has to offer—which is, coincidentally, the condensation of his father's career: a classically trained academicism founded on fine drawing technique. *All the better to mirror nature, my dear!*

Rebel without a Cause

By 1897, the 16-year-old Picasso is bored with the restraints of academicism and drops out of La Lonja. He heads for the **bohemian life of Madrid,** where, in record time, he brilliantly passes the entrance exam at the Royal Academy of San Fernando. Since he has little money and few friends, he spends hours at the Prado, copying paintings by Velázquez and Goya and studying the works of **Vincent van Gogh** (1853–1890) and **Paul Cézanne** (1839–1906). It's a tough life, though, and by spring 1898 he contracts scarlet fever, which prompts a return to Barcelona. Early in the summer, his old friend from La Lonja, **Manuel Pallardés,** invites him to convalesce at his family home in the village of Horta. There, Picasso enjoys drawing the locals, but he also learns to tend sheep, press olive oil, and shoot a rifle like a marksman. He becomes fluent in Catalan, the dialect of Catalonia (and Salvador Dalí's native language), and the two friends spend part of their eight months together living in a cave in the mountains, an early experience with "primitivism."

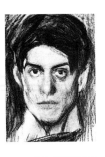

Self-Portrait. 1900
Charcoal on gray
paper, 8 ⁷/₈ x 6 ¹/₂"
(22.5 x 16.5 cm)

In February 1899, Picasso returns to Barcelona and drops into the city's bohemian culture. He makes the scene at **Els Quatre Gats** (Catalan for "The Four Cats"), a café where poets, painters, musicians, intellectuals, and rebels convene. There, he becomes friends with the painter **Carlos Casagemas** (1880–1901) and the poet **Jaime Sabartés** (1881–1968). Between lively bouts of wine-guzzling and marathon discussions into the wee hours with friends, the 18-year-old artist puts together his first solo show on February 1, 1900.

The Last Moments, a painting from his solo exhibition, is chosen for exhibition in the Paris Universal Exhibition (of Eiffel Tower fame). Picasso and Casagemas travel to Paris in October 1900 and find a small studio in Montmartre, where they mingle with the Spanish colony of artists and begin to make connections. At the time, Paris is the epicenter of the art world (and will continue to be so until the 1950s, when the Abstract Expressionists shift the focus to New York). Before long, two dealers—**Berthe Weill** and **Pedro Mañach**—express interest in Picasso's work, and, for the first time, Picasso is able to earn a living from the sale of his art.

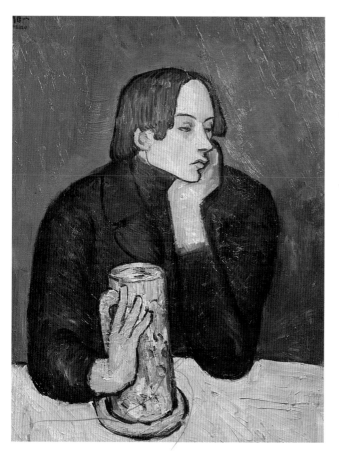

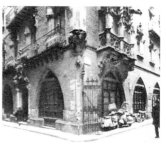

ABOVE
*Els Quatre
Gats, Barcelona*

LEFT
*Portrait of Jaime
Sabartés.* 1901
32 ¹/₄ x 26"
(82 x 66 cm)

Pushkin Museum of Fine Arts,
Moscow, Russia. Giraudon/
Art Resource, NY

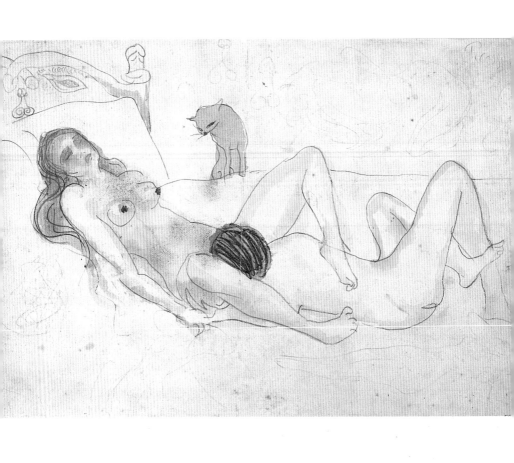

But his good fortune lasts only a year. He and Casagemas return to Barcelona in December 1900 for a brief interlude, then head back to Paris. Tragically, Casagemas finds himself impotent with the woman of his dreams, the model Germaine, and commits suicide in February 1901. The shock of Casagemas's death *(flash!)* kicks Picasso into gear and initiates the Blue Period.

But First, Some Cultural Background

Up to now, Picasso has spent his time in Paris getting up to speed. Basically, this consists of familiarizing himself with the established culture of Impressionism (urban themes; quasi-scientific attempts to represent fleeting perceptions; dappled brushwork and colors) and of exploring the experimental possibilities of **Post-Impressionism.** These possibilities are on every modern mind, with a spate of important exhibitions of work by Van Gogh, Cézanne, and **Paul Gauguin** (1848–1903) at the beginning of the century. Picasso does a quick study of the situation and shows a fondness for:

- **Henri de Toulouse-Lautrec** (1864–1901): Picasso shares this artist's predilection for Parisian low life (cabarets, brothels, circuses) and racy caricature.

- **Pierre-Auguste Renoir** (1841–1919): Picasso's experiments yield grotesque renditions of this Impressionist's work by turning Renoir's petted beauties into rich old hags and his famous "rainbow palette"

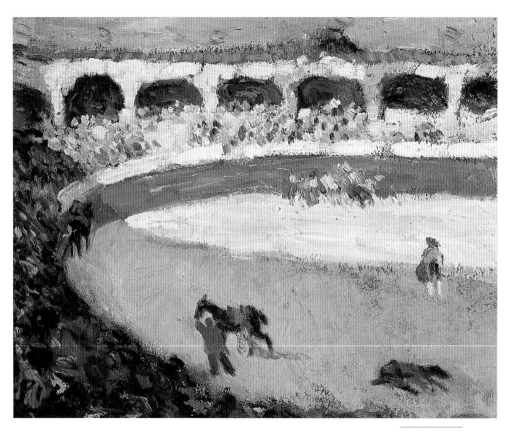

Bullfight. 1901

Private Collection. Scala/
Art Resource, NY

into a hail of luridly colored brushstrokes.

- **Art Nouveau:** As cofounder and art editor for the Catalan review, *Arte Joven,* Picasso shows how marvelously stylized his work can be and demonstrates a taste for graphic as well as fine arts.

Baby's Got the Blues: The Blue Period (1901–04)

It takes a few months to register, but when Casagemas's suicide hits, it hits hard. To date, Picasso has signed most of his work "P. Ruiz" or "P. Ruiz Picasso," but now begins to use only his last name. In May, Picasso moves into the dead poet's (no doubt spooky) ex-studio and by September his work has taken a decided turn. Just compare his self-portraits. *Yo Picasso* (on page 35) shows him in the spring of 1901, the confident dandy who flings colors around and wears orange accessories. Later that same year, he's the completely buttoned-up, modern bohemian in a black coat, framing a haunted expression, cast in cold blue light. Welcome to the Blue Period! Here's what to look for:

- **El Greco** (1541–1614): The Blue Period begins with Picasso's painting, *Evocation (The Burial of*

BACKTRACK IMPRESSIONISM

Based in Paris, the Impressionists (also known as the New Painters) attempted to almost scientifically represent their *perceptions* of the **transient effects of light and movement** on the visual world. Dappled brushwork dissolves into atmospheric compositions and vibrant colors, *rendering a "realism" of the moment.* They were motivated by naturalism, but introduced a concept of painting based on extreme artifice that transferred attention from external subjects (nature) to **subjective perceptions** (the artist's eye). This is what makes Impressionism so essential to the development of Modernism: It grants the possibilities for abstraction.

Casagemas), an homage to the Spanish painter El Greco's *The Burial of Count Orgaz* (1586), an angelic ascension to heaven. But, as befits a modern tragedy, *Evocation* stars a new cast that includes a flock of whores, who see Casagemas off on his journey into the clouds. The hallmark mannerisms of Picasso's Blue Period—namely the blue palette and attenuated, slender figures— refer also to El Greco.

- **Melancholy and depression:** Populated by beggars and bar flies, these paintings really do have the blues. With all the warmth of humanity drained out of them, these pictures are chilly with death and sadness. Psychologically speaking, they are nearly suicidal.

- **Alienation and life's futility:** Images of blindness express Picasso's own fear of being visually silenced. In *La Vie,* painted in 1903 while Picasso is back in Barcelona for a few months, a young woman clings to Casagemas, who waives a negating finger at another woman with a baby in her arms. The sadness these figures express comes from a sense of alienation between individuals who, even when they're seated side by side in a café, cannot connect with one another. Notice how the people in the Blue-Period paintings hold their arms so closely to their sides: They are emotionally and physically straight-jacketed, unable to participate fully in life. *La Celestina,* featuring the one-eyed madam from Fernando de Roja's play, is painted during the same productive season, as is the "mannerist" work *The Old Guitarist.*

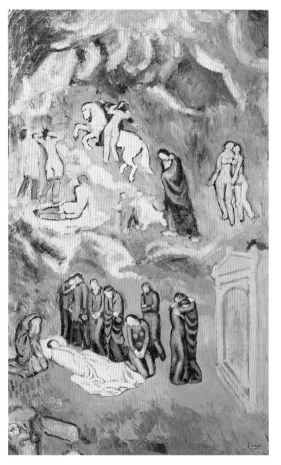

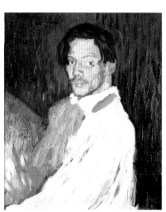

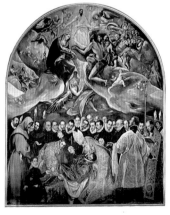

La Celestina
1903
31 ⁷/₈ x 23 ⁵/₈"
(81 x 60 cm)

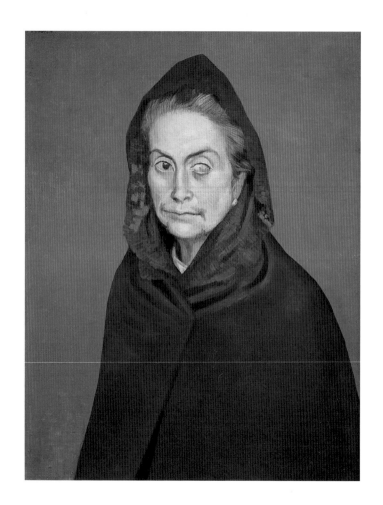

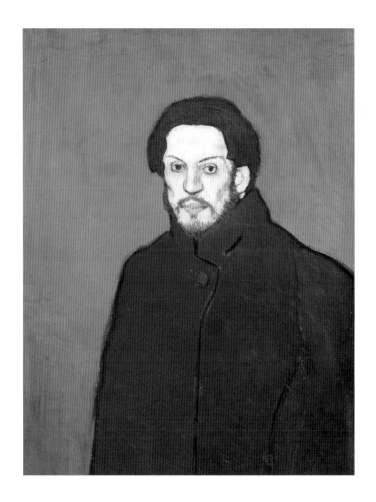

Self-Portrait. 1901
31 $^1/_2$ x 23 $^5/_8$"
(80 x 60 cm)

Musée Picasso, Paris, France.
Giraudon/Art Resource, NY

LA VIE, 1903
77 ³/₈ x 50 ⁵/₈" (196.5 x 128.5 cm)

Cleveland Museum of Art, Cleveland, Ohio, U.S.A. Giraudon/Art Resource, NY

What was he thinking? About life's futility.

Qu'est-ce que c'est? An allegorical image starring Picasso's friend, Carlos Casagemas, whose death by suicide seems to have precipitated the deeply sad Blue-Period paintings. This period is perfectly represented by *La Vie*.

Hopeless reincarnation: Casagemas appears returned to the land of the living, only to take a stand against life itself. A young woman clings to him. They form a sexual couple, but he waives his finger "no" to the image of motherhood that stands before them. It's not that he doesn't like babies: The baby who sleeps in its mother's arms is sweet and important. It's *life* that is horrendous, terrible, and sad.

Sadness galore! Chilly colors, bloodless flesh, stony expressions, frozen gestures: Every inch of this picture is drenched in *sadness and impotence.*

The writing on the walls: There is a pair of images between the two couples expressed as sketches tacked to the wall. These images distill, picture-in-a-picture style, what the larger sadness is about. A couple clutches together; a man crouches with his head down. They seem to say, "There is no hope in love and regeneration. There is only solitude and suffering."

Sad note strikes smashing success for Spain: Shortly after this painting was completed, its sale ("for a respectable price") to a prominent Parisian collector made news back home in Spain. In a "local boy makes good" piece of journalism, the Barcelona newspaper *El Liberal* proudly reported that *La Vie* was "one of those works which, even considering it apart from the rest, can establish the reputation and name of an artist."

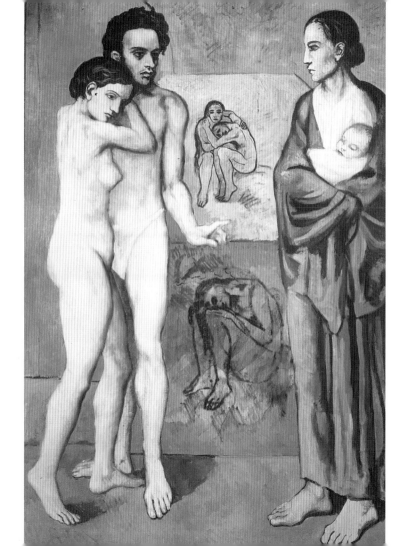

POST-IMPRESSIONISM

Attempts to depict subjective reality by transforming the traditional stuff of representational painting—perspective, color, line—**into abstract or symbolic expressions.** Typical subject matter: nature and an idealized life within it. Not members of a movement *per se*, the Post-Impressionists worked separately from one another to formulate, during the 1880s, independent paths out of Impressionism and the Realist/Naturalist tradition. The key figures are:

Paul Cézanne (1839–1906) had *the most profound impact on Picasso.* When you see faceted planes or surfaces, think Cézanne. He envisioned the world in terms of delicately structured surfaces that simultaneously describe volume, perspective, and light. He lived like a hermit in Aix-en-Provence, in the South of France, and worked in relative obscurity. His impact on the avant-garde was delayed until 1895, when the dealer **Ambroise Vollard** (1868–1939) showed his paintings, which would galvanize generations to follow (most dramatically, the Cubists). What they responded to was Cézanne's attempt to reconcile the *imperfect world of perception* with the substance that he knew to exist underlying those perceptions. The resulting images—clumsy and cerebral at once—give bony structure to something as ephemeral as light.

Paul Gauguin (1848–1903) advocated *drawing from memory and imagination,* and spent a lifetime in search of a primitive paradise in which to realize his vision.

Vincent van Gogh (1853–1890) attempted to communicate the *emotional intensity* with which he observed life through the use of exaggerated color, forceful design, and vividly rendered drawing.

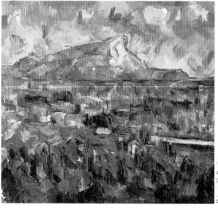

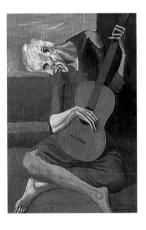

LEFT
The Old Guitarist
1903. Oil and canvas
47 3/4 x 32 1/2"
(121.3 x 82.5 cm)

The Art Institute of Chicago, Helen
Birch Bartlett Memorial Collection

OPPOSITE
Paul Cézanne
*Mont Sainte
Victoire.* 1904–06
25 1/2 x 32"
(65 x 81 cm)

The trouble with Picasso's blues is that we have this twenty-something artist, who's already being touted as the next hot thing, wallowing in gloom about the human condition, when he's hardly experienced life himself. Even though he is living the life of a poor bohemian, these pictures, with their pronounced mannerisms and Symbolist angst, can appear a tad self-indulgent, even cloying. But, having mastered a new expression, Picasso is ready to move on.

FYI: **Blindness**—A recurrent motif in the Blue-Period paintings is the image of blindness, which reveals Picasso's own fears of being visually silenced.

**BACKTRACK
SYMBOLISM**

More a literary movement than an artistic one, Symbolism originates in the poetry of **Stéphane Mallarmé** (1842–1898) and other late-19th-century writers. According to the Symbolist manifesto of 1895, it aimed to represent life's intangibles through associative images and colors: "to clothe the idea in sensuous form." Looking beyond everyday realities ("how to draw an apple") to subjective concerns ("how to represent sexual terror"), Symbolism can conjure **mysticism and decadence.** As a late-19th-century ethos, it can also be seen as an essential engine for Modernism—certainly for young Picasso—in that it promoted an expressionist art based on abstract and psychological concepts.

La Vie en Rose: *The Rose Period* (1904–06)

In the spring of 1904, Picasso, who has been shuttling between Paris and Barcelona, settles in Paris. He moves into a studio building at 13, rue Ravignan, known as **Le Bateau-Lavoir** (i.e., the Laundry Boat), where he meets **Fernande Olivier.** She will be his mistress for the next seven years. By winter, his art begins to take on greater naturalism and a rosier hue. The Rose-Period pictures are **images of circus life,** as Picasso idealizes it based on his sometimes thrice-weekly visits to the Cirque Médrano—a *bona fide* circus located at the bottom of the hilly Montmartre, where Picasso likes to hobnob with the clowns between acts. He sees in the itinerant band of artists **an alternative family made up of misfits and monkeys.** Although life is still a little sad and marginal, it seems less terrifying now to Picasso. Women are no longer prostitutes, but glowing young mothers. Picasso allots the leading role to **Harlequin, the artist**—a private and introverted person who must publicly act the clown. Picasso's Harlequin is one of his first expressions of the **alienation** that plagues and inspires the artist for his entire career.

Le Bateau-Lavoir

This decrepit wood building with its labyrinthine plan and smelly, graffitied hallways had housed artists since 1892, when a painter friend of Paul Gauguin's, Maufra, took a studio there and made it a meeting place for artists, anarchists, and Symbolist sympathizers. Located on what was then the almost rustic outskirts of Paris, Montmartre offered lodgings that artists could afford. Picasso's residence in this building makes it legendary: **Max Jacob** (1876–1944), fellow resident and poet, dubs it the "Acropolis of Cubism," but also calls it "The Laundry Boat," a moniker that sticks. When not working in their studios, the artists of Montmartre hang out at a café called **Le Lapin Agile,** whose bohemian owner, Frédé, keeps a pet donkey named Lolo. (This donkey later scandalizes the art world in 1910 when a canvas "painted" by her with her paint-dipped tail is included in a Salon exhibition under the name of Boronalis.) Fernande Olivier later recalls that this artistic circle had a penchant for "deep conversation inspired by opium."

Sound Byte:

"There was a box mattress on four legs in the corner... a cane chair, easels, canvases of all sizes, paint tubes scattered on the floor with paint brushes.... There were no curtains. In the winter, it was so bitter cold that the tea remaining in the cups from the night before was frozen in the morning."
—FERNANDE OLIVIER, describing Picasso's
studio at the Bateau-Lavoir

FYI: The Bateau-Lavoir burned down on May 12, 1970.

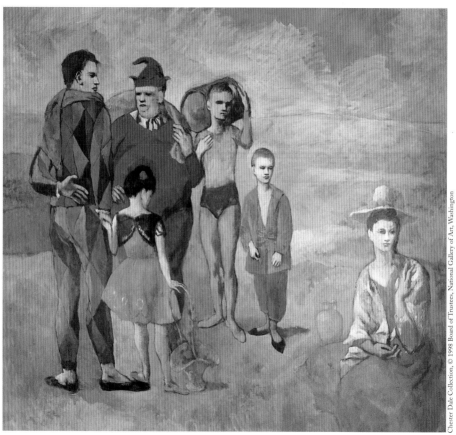

From Roses to Stones

The Family of Saltimbanques, Picasso's major Rose-Period picture, exemplifies his talent for transforming personal matters into a larger evocation of human isolation. Set in a blasted-pink dream space, the picture begins as a series of portraits—including that of the poet and critic **Guillaume Apollinaire** (1880 –1918) as a fat jester—but turns into an assembly of figures who forge an ironic sense of community out of their mutual detachment. A woman on the edge of the group, modeled after Fernande, previews the way in which Picasso's imagery of women changes as he moves out of the Rose Period—from rosy maternal figures to mysterious, self-absorbed sphinxes more interested in coiffure than in kids. **Already, he's looking to create archetypal figures or *types* within his art**—images that can elicit a particular response even if you don't know the specific reference. To achieve the desired **air of detachment,** he moves away from cafés and contemporary culture and models his work on ancient classical art. (Later you'll see how Picasso draws on Primitivism and Neoclassicism to achieve similar measures of distance in his otherwise completely contemporary art.) *Woman with a Fan* is as hardened as an Egyptian profile, from which it seemingly derives. The Rose Period proves popular among critics and buyers and wins for Picasso an important patron, the author **Gertrude Stein** (1874–1946), who will write a portrait essay of the young artist. In 1906, he sets about painting her.

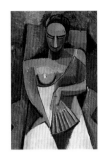

Woman with a Fan. 1908

Hermitage, St. Petersburg, Russia.
Scala/Art Resource, NY

OPPOSITE
Family of Saltimbanques
1905
83 ³/₄ x 90 ³/₈"
(212.8 x 229.6 cm)

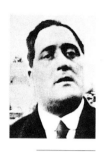

*Guillaume
Apollinaire*
before 1914

Painting Gertrude

She sits and sits and sits some more, and after 80 or 90 sittings, Picasso still can't put a face on Gertrude Stein. In frustration, he wipes down the upper part of the portrait with turpentine and grabs Fernande for a holiday in Spain. In the Pyrénées, he experiences **a vivid connection (flash!) with the Iberian stone sculptures** from the Andalusian region of Spain that he had seen that spring at the Louvre museum. He returns to Paris and in one sitting solves what's wrong with Gertrude's head *by painting her in the manner of an Iberian sculpture!* When friends see her thus transformed into an incredible brown hulk of unclassical beauty with a stony mask of a face, they say: "But Gertrude doesn't look like that." Picasso responds, **"She will."**

Sound Byte:

"He gave me the picture and I was and I still am satisfied with my portrait, for me, it is I, and it is the only reproduction of me which is always I, for me."
—GERTRUDE STEIN, describing her portrait by Picasso

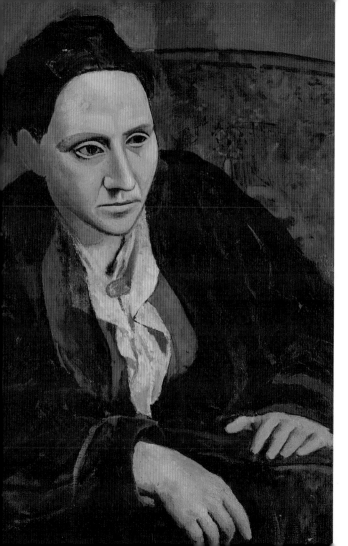

PORTRAIT OF GERTRUDE STEIN, 1905–06
39 ³/₈ x 32" (100 x 81.3 cm)

American writer living in Paris who penned the Modernist mantra: "A rose is a rose is a rose." In her Montparnasse apartment at 27, rue de Fleurus, Stein presided over an **epicenter of avant-gardism,** attracting to her regular Saturday salons the painters Picasso and Matisse; the writer **Ernest Hemingway** (1899–1961); and the composer **Virgil Thomson** (1896–1989), among other luminaries. Stein's companion, **Alice B. Toklas** (1877–1967), was an amazing cook, as renowned for her pot brownies as for her fish aspics, the latter decorated after Picasso.

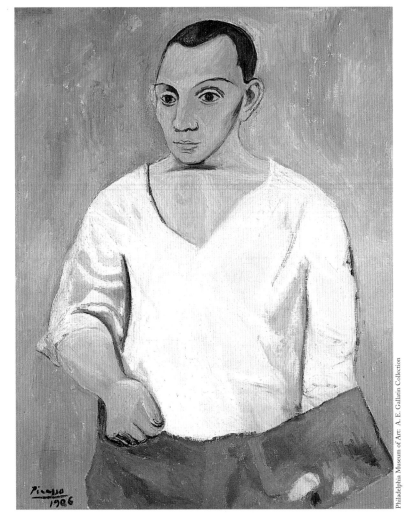

Self-Portrait with a Palette. 1906
36 ¹/₄ x 28 ³/₄"
(92 x 73 cm)

Cheeky Monkey!

Stein loves her Picasso portrait and she *does* come to resemble this emblematic image. (Check out any subsequent photo.) Rude though it may sound, **Picasso's assertion is a major claim for Modernism:** *From now on, instead of copying nature and mirroring reality, artists must create their own realities.* One look at Picasso's 1906 *Self-Portrait with a Palette* proves him the man for the job. Compared to the paralyzed Blue-Period aesthete of five years earlier, Pablo is rejuvenated. He holds a palette of paint and wears work clothes that show off his thick, muscular body. His stony expression, like Stein's, masks his inner being. He's impenetrable—fortified to make art and to construct new realities.

The Plot Thickens

The annual autumn Salon of 1905 had been one of Modernism's big hooplas, because it unleashed **Fauvism,** which loudly rejected naturalistic representation in favor of *a purely sensual use of color.* Led by Henri Matisse, the Fauves didn't appear to have any immediate impact on Picasso's art. (Typically, he was not persuaded by what he himself had not discovered or had not had a leading role in.) He dismissed their work as decorative. But when Picasso meets Matisse at Gertrude Stein's in the spring of 1906 and Matisse shows him an African carving he has just purchased, Picasso is impressed. He begins

French for "wild beasts,"
Fauves are what critic Louis
Vauxcelles called the artists
led by Henri Matisse, who
showed their crudely
rendered, colorful paintings
in the 1905 Autumn Salon.
Considered **the first avant-
garde art movement of
the 20th century,** Fauvism
was short-lived: 1905 to
1908. Its main claim to fame
was the painters' use of color
to create emotional, spatial,
and decorative effects.
Other Fauves include
Georges Braque
(1882–1963),
André Derain
(1880–1954), and
Maurice de Vlaminck
(1876–1958).

sketching what will become possibly the most radical picture of the 20th century, *Les Demoiselles d'Avignon*, a direct response to Matisse's Fauvist masterpiece, *Le Bonheur de vivre*. Matisse's work is a paradise tableau, framed by trees, populated by lolling and frolicking nudes of both sexes. Picasso's response to it chews up the scenery.

FYI: Not to be outdone, Matisse responds to Cubism by holding out against "Picasso's movement" and not becoming directly involved with its issues.

Picasso's Primitivism

The impact of tribal art and artifacts on Picasso's work (and on Modernism in general) cannot be overstated. Here's what to know about Picasso's Primitivism:

- Sometime in May or June of 1907, he visits the ethnographic museum at the Palais du Trocadéro, where **he sees African sculpture** and experiences *(flash!)* a revelation. He runs back to his studio and repaints the heads of three of the *Demoiselles*, his final work on the painting.

- He's not the first to discover Primitivism. By 1907, most of the Fauves have been collecting tribal art and finding inspiration in it.

- Picasso's Primitivism shows affinities with African and Oceanic art. Warning: It's dangerous to start attributing Picassoid abstractions to specific African sculptures without knowing more about the history of those works. For example, even though the face on the far right *looks* like a mask from the Etombi region of the People's Republic of the Congo, we know that no objects from this region reached France until years after Picasso had completed the *Demoiselles.* It is certain, however, that he would have seen examples of Kota and Hongwe reliquary figures at the Trocadéro; they were common enough to be turning up at the time in curiosity shops. Distinguished by the often highly abstract patterns of stripes and hatchmarks that cover their face, these figures made a large impression on Picasso's *Demoiselles.*

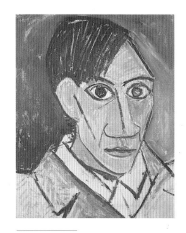

Self-Portrait. 1907
19 3/4 x 18 1/8"
(50 x 46 cm)

National Gallery, Prague,
Czech Republic. Giraudon/
Art Resource, NY

According to Picasso, the two things he found most exciting about African art were:

- **Its sense of magic:** He saw in tribal art the power to exorcise — to dominate reality and change it.

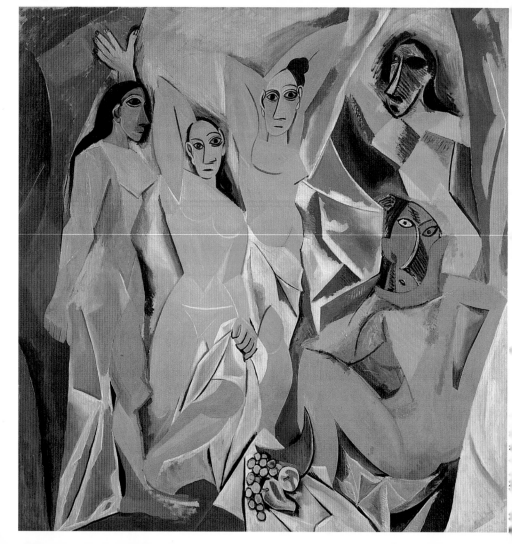

LES DEMOISELLES D'AVIGNON, 1907
8' x 7'8" (243.9 x 233.7 cm)

Subject: Five women (yes, those are women) and a fruit dish (in the center foreground). The composition is like a stage, with the figure on the left pulling back a curtain and presenting (*yikes!*) her companions.

The title: "The Young Ladies of Avignon" refers to the denizens of a famous redlight district in Barcelona, located along Avignon Street; the painting's original title was *The Avignon Bordello*. (The name does not refer to the city in southern France.)

Perhaps the most shocking image in 20th-century art: "It was as if he had asked us to eat rope and drink gasoline," said one of Picasso's peers about the painting.

Style: One of the most radical innovations of this painting is the stylistic conflict it embodies: Instead of having one style, it has many. The faces of the women present the most obvious **differences in style.** Their heads appear jammed onto their bodies as if they have come to a (costumeless) Hallowe'en party wearing different masks. The two in the center with the great staring eyes facing directly out of the picture (and who appear most normal to our eyes) resemble Picasso's contemporary **images based on ancient Iberian sculpture.** The other three, however, are each different takes on Picasso's experi-ence with **African tribal art** (more about this in a moment). The left half of the painting is reminiscent of his Rose Period, but the right half , with its rich colors and striated faces, is (in dealer Daniel-Henry Kahnweiler's words) "the starting point of a new art." The repre-sentation of space adheres to several different systems simultaneously. Notice the way the figure squatting on the lower right appears to be seen strangely in the round (her body is like a butterflied, boneless breast of chicken). But the two figures in the center are com-pletely frontal. If this were a film, the camera would be sometimes moving, sometimes still. But this is a painting and **many viewpoints are being seen at once.** The painting is also incomplete. Look at the woman's leg on the far left: It's been sketched over as if Picasso intended to rework it, but he never did. It's as if there are so many styles that it would be impossible to synthesize them into a cohesive image. The harmony of this painting is *disharmony*.

What was he thinking? About distortions of tribal African sculpture and exorcism. With this painting, Picasso *wanted* to make the viewer feel unsettled.

Big nudes: It began with Picasso wanting to make a major painting in response to all the big nudes of his time. These included

Cézanne's *Large Bathers*, which everyone was looking at, and pictorial statements issued by Fauvists Matisse and Derain—all large-scale nudes. They were all set in ambiguous woodland glades, but Picasso wanted *his* nudes to evoke Barcelona's seamy waterfront district.

Paul Cézanne: Picasso copped more than just the monumental scale of his figures from the Post-Impressionist Cézanne: The figures' poses and the way they are situated in space, as if seen from many angles at once, are direct references to Cézanne (although it seems that Picasso was also cribbing from a postcard image of a group of Sudanese women that was recently discovered in his archive). The volumes of this picture (the bodies and spaces in between them) are also depicted with Cézanne in mind: The latter had deployed a new way of seeing the complex volume of a picture that involved **breaking it down into simple geometric shapes** and fitting the shapes deliberately back together. Picasso seems to break up the image with a hammer and leave the shards scattered disruptively across the surface.

The original cast: The painting evolved over months of drawing and reworking. Early sketches show how Picasso started with a little morality play, enacted by a cast of characters that included tempting prostitutes, a sailor randy to do business, and a medical student mindfully shrinking from the sins of the flesh and rampant venereal disease. To reinforce the fatal last point, Picasso toys around with a skull as part of the still-life props.

African epiphany: As he worked on the picture, Picasso increasingly suppressed the allegorical and moral content so that all that remains of the original cast are the nudes. Their depiction shrieks of an encounter that changed Picasso's entire concept of painting. In the midst of working on this painting, he paid a visit to the Palais du Trocadéro, the local ethnography museum, where **he experienced a sense of magic in African sculpture** that he wanted his own art to possess. He saw objects imbued with the power of exorcism—the power to give form to fear and, by so doing, to *conquer fear*.

Confrontational art: So now, instead of making a little allegory of his sexual fear (the scary whores, the performance anxieties, the threat of disease, etc.), Picasso made a picture that *embodied* his fear. That's what makes this painting so profound: *The threat of sexuality is now the threat of the picture itself.*

It's not just that figures are frightening *images* of women, but that the entire surface of the picture is made to appear spiky and dangerous. Iberian masks collide with African ones and the surface is impaled with references to Cézanne. The unfinished state in which Picasso left the painting only compounds **the sense of menace, disorientation, and threat** that these strange combinations imply. Picasso enjoins us, as viewers, to *confront* these fears, which his painting causes us not only to envision, but to experience and overcome. The painting poses as an imagery of initiation, or a rite of passage. After seeing *Demoiselles* in all its shocking glory, you should feel confident—and not afraid—to take on anything that Modern art has to offer.

Cubist or Expressionist? Shortly after (nearly) completing it, Picasso rolled up *Demoiselles* and stowed it in his studio. It did not go on public view until the late 1930s, when it was purchased by The Museum of Modern Art in New York and was deemed "the first monument of Cubism." However, given that it was essentially out of circulation, the painting really stands outside of the Cubist formulation, especially when one considers that the emotional content and shrill, shrieking pitch of this frightening and disjointed picture is distinctively unlike anything one finds in Cubism. Thus, it is not wrong to call *Demoiselles* an Expressionist painting. After all, it's the expression of sex and fear we're talking about here, not of little cubes. *This painting wants to eat you alive!*

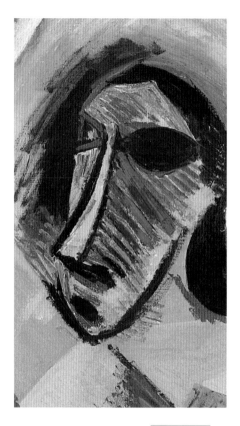

Detail from
*Les Demoiselles
d'Avignon*

- **A form of affirmation:** What he encounters in African sculpture is pictorial affirmation: It makes his bizarre new tendencies look perfectly reasonable. He calls it "reasonable," which seems at odds with magical. But by the time Picasso has his Trocadéro *(flash!)* revelation, he has already started dismantling and amplifying his own gestures and mannerisms. He turns, say, cross-hatching, which he's been taught shadows a form and gives it volume, into crazy stripes that just sit on top of a face. African sculpture seems to call out, "Chop loose those ties to Western tradition and go for something more Modern…say, Cubism."

Sound Byte:

"If you give spirits a shape, you break free from them… I grasped why I was a painter. All alone in that museum, surrounded by masks, Red Indian Dolls, dummies covered with dust. Demoiselles *must have come that day: not at all because of their forms. No, but because it was my first exorcising painting."*

—PICASSO, describing his revelation
at the Trocadéro museum, Paris.

From Strange to Stone-Age Women

The spiky *Demoiselles* are replaced by the lumpy *Three Women*. They are a trogolodyte take on the classical three graces, slow-moving and landlocked in a solid shallow space, colored in subdued terra-cotta and cedar tones. In moving away from the primitivist prostitutes to these primal forms, Picasso is really pushing the dial backward on the old time machine. And he's not the only one. Concurrently, the Swiss linguist **Ferdinand de Saussure** (1857–1913) is arguing that the first human conversation around the earliest campfires wasn't just a matter of mimicking natural sounds. Language, he says, originates in the power of the human brain to invent arbitrary symbols imbued with meaning. It doesn't *refer* to an outside, real world; language exists in its own interior world of signs and meanings. This new theory relates directly to what Picasso (along with other Modernists, such as his good friend Gertrude Stein) is doing: He's trying to **break art down to its essential grammar of elements** that are meaningless in themselves and only gain meaning from the context in which the artist puts them and from their relationship to one another. In going back to primitive and primal beginnings (and beyond the classical beginnings of Western culture), Modernists are creating a new theory of evolution, in which artists aren't slaves to nature.

**BACKTRACK
EXPRESSIONISM**

A modern metamorphosis of the Symbolist sensibility. Responding to the work of Van Gogh and of **Edvard Munch** (1863–1944), among others, the Expressionists aimed to make their work convey a particular emotion or sensation—and they readily resorted to whatever exaggerations and distortions were necessary. **Fauvism is considered the first Expressionist movement,** an antecedent to German Expressionism, which came into existence after World War I.

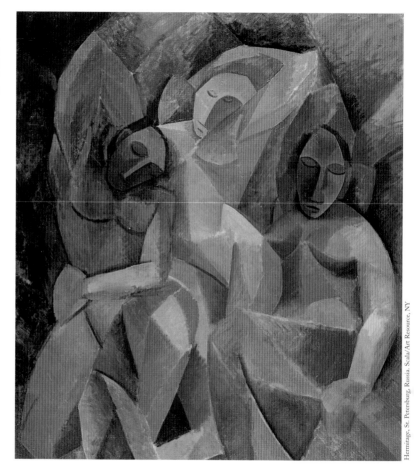

Three Women
1908
78 ³/₄ x 70 ¹/₈"
(200 x 178 cm)

They've got the power to conceptualize, create, and dominate systems of visual representation. *Who knew that these three galumphing ladies were into such smart stuff?*

In November 1908, Pablo and Fernande throw a banquet honoring the primitivist artist, **Henri Rousseau** (1844–1910). It's a burlesque affair in the shabby old Bateau-Lavoir, with such guests as Gertrude Stein, Apollinaire, and Braque (with whom Picasso is becoming good friends). Having just purchased Rousseau's *Portrait of a Woman*, Picasso offers this toast: "You and I are the greatest painters of our time, you in the Egyptian style, I in the Modern." Picasso admires the simplicity of Rousseau's art, which leads him to *(flash!)* sharpen and clarify his own. In 1909, he paints a series of still lifes that bring together Rousseau's sweetly solid forms and Cézanne's complex faceted space. Having synthesized consolidation with dissolution, **he's ready to move on to Cubism.**

Ah, Cubism (1908–14)

Cubism came, historically, just after Fauvism and was the next major innovation in Modern art. It, too, was named by the critic Louis Vauxcelles, who described

**BACKTRACK
PRIMITIVISM**

A major phenomenon of Modernism. Cultures outside of the direct impact of Western society and technology (what we like to think of as *civilization*) were considered to be in their childhoods and, thus, ripe for being dominated and plundered. Van Gogh's interest in Japanese art, Gauguin's in Oceanic, and Picasso's in African are all forms of Primitivism. In each case, the artist celebrates what he perceives as **simpler means of representation,** potentially **new forms of abstraction,** and/or just plain **magic.** Consequently, Westerners stomp over the original context and complexities of their sources in favor of self-serving agendas. That's the trouble with Primitivism: Its sources are not in formative or degenerative stages of our culture; they *are* their own cultures.

Also known as *Le Douanier*
Rousseau because of his
day job as a customs agent
(*douanier* is French for
"customs officer"), Rousseau
took up painting as a hobby
and ended up being one of
the first Primitives of Modern
Art. Unschooled, his ambition
was to paint in the grand
tradition; his personal naïveté
was one of the charms that
attracted the critic Apollinaire,
who turned Picasso, among
others, on to his work. They
admired the lucid simplicity
of Rousseau's vision, its
dreamlike clarity.

what he saw in a 1908 exhibition of paintings by
Georges Braque: "[He] reduces everything, places and
figures and houses, to geometric schemes, to cubes."
And from that, the term *Cubist* was born. (It's interest-
ing to note that there are not "cubes" *per se* in the
paintings, just boxy edges.) By 1909, the term "Cubism"
was in common use. Unlike the Fauvists (who were
ever-so-history-conscious), the Cubists were convinced
that the tradition of painting was useless to truly
contemporary sensibilities. As evolved by Picasso and
Braque, **Cubism sought a completely conceptual
interpretation of reality.** It *assassinated* the naturalist
tradition, as represented by Impressionism. The Cubist
world (modeled with devotion on Cézanne's) was a
return to basics: geometric forms, neutral colors (only
late Cubism admits the use of rich colors), and minimal
technique (there's not a lot of bravado brushwork in
Cubism). Space, however, was a wreck, producing many
simultaneous points of view. The agitated surfaces of
Cubist pictures appear to emerge on impact between
angular linear fragments and massive volumes. In pick-
ing out the imagery, the viewer of a Cubist painting
becomes a co-creator of the picture by putting it
together like a puzzle, just as the artist did to begin

with. This new relationship between artist and viewer is another major innovation in Modern art. Cubism is divided into two phases: **Analytic Cubism** and **Synthetic Cubism**. One of its greatest discoveries is **collage**.

Picasso "Joins" Cubism

That's right: Cubism does not originate with Picasso. That distinction belongs to Georges Braque, who comes up with the new ideas while working closely with Picasso, who responds with inspiring imagination. Only six months apart in age, Braque and Picasso meet in 1907 and could not be more different in temperament:

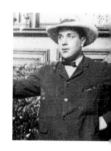

Georges Braque

Braque is 25 years old:

- He is affiliated with the **Fauves** and is just beginning to claim attention for his work.

- A **methodical** artist, his paintings are tentative and controlled; he *works slowly* and deliberately.

- He is influenced by Cézanne, with whom he identifies so strongly that, in 1908, he starts to wear the same style of domed hat that Cézanne wore.

Picasso is 26 years old:

- He has established himself as a hot young property with his **Rose-Period** works.

- A **volatile** talent, he is a quick to assimilate things that interest him and to dominate them in his work.

- He is thinking about mashing Cézanne with Primitivism.

Cézanne was an influential figure on Cubism, not to mention that his work was the subject of a major memorial retrospective in Paris in 1907, just as the potential for Cubism began to percolate in Braque's and Picasso's art.

Parallel Courses

Picasso works on *Les Demoiselles d'Avignon*, and Braque (who rarely includes figures in his work) demonstrates his admiration by painting, in the spring of 1908, a monumental nude. He responds to Picasso by combining several points of view at once, but sticks to Cézanne when he makes the background a complex system of interlocking planes. That same summer, Braque applies his new sense of mass and space to a series of landscapes painted in the southern French town of

L'Estaque. When he submits them for exhibition in the Fall Salon, the jury (purportedly led by Matisse, who turns up his nose at all those "little cubes") gives them the thumbs down. The dealer **Daniel-Henry Kahnweiler** (1884–1976), however, gives them a show.

Ready for Impact

In the meantime, it becomes clear in 1909, when the two men return to Paris from separate summer vacations in the south, that they are working on nearly identical issues. Braque has painted provincial architecture of ruins on hillsides associated with Cézanne. He begins to break up the contours of his forms in anticipation of future developments of Cubism based on increasingly complex *passage* (French for "passages," a key term in Cubism used to describe the links between foreground and background planes; the more objects and spaces dissolve into one another, the more complex the *passage*). Picasso, on the other hand, has vacationed in Horta del Ebro (now called Horta de San Juan), Spain, and has painted a small factory town in which organic and manmade plants ambiguously merge. He thus makes his first fully defined works of Cubism: landscapes in which the town, trees, and mountains are painted as sculpted forms in shallow relief.

The results, established mostly by Braque, are **Analytic Cubism.** This first phase of Cubism focuses on traditional studio and landscape

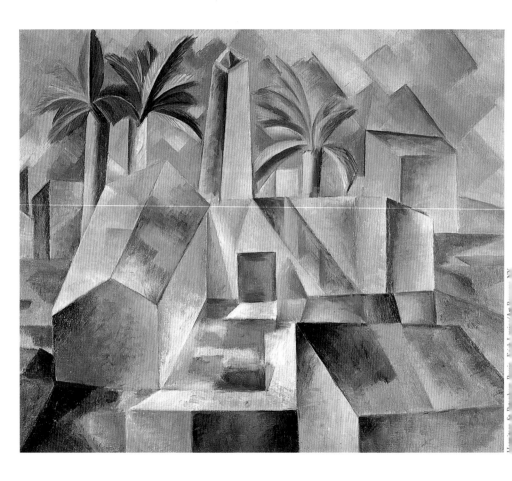

subjects. The palette is stripped down to **neutral tones,** almost like the colors of drawings. Masses and spaces are unified in a relatively **sculptural relief.** There is no single vantage point (perspective bobs all over the place) and large masses become sheer planes, with light emanating from no particular source.

Heads and More Heads

Picasso thinks about translating into a bronze sculpture the Cubist portraits he has painted of Fernande that summer. He hopes to **shatter** a solid form with *radiating fields of energy,* but the resulting *Head of a Woman* (it's Fernande!) brings him up against the limitations of traditional sculpture in relation to his new thinking. The material is simply too dense to convey the idea of dissolution he's exploring in Cubism. In September 1909, based on the financial success of his recent exhibition, Picasso and Fernande move to fancier digs (with a maid!) at 11, boulevard de Clichy. In his new studio, Picasso embarks on a **series of unprecedented portraits.**

The Cubist Portraits of 1910

He begins with the portrait of a *Girl with a Mandolin,* which is left unfinished after the model, Fanny Tellier, quits, and **paints portraits of the dealers Daniel-Henry Kahnweiler, Ambroise Vollard,** and **Wilhelm Uhde.** These remarkable Cubist portraits are:

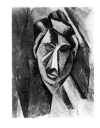

Head of a Woman
1909. Gouache
24 $^5/_8$ x 18 $^1/_2$"
(62.5 x 47 cm)

OPPOSITE
Factory at Horta de Hero. 1909
20 $^7/_8$ x 23 $^1/_2$"
(53 x 60 cm)

Portrait of Daniel-Henry Kahnweiler. 1910
39 5/8 x 25 5/8"
(100.6 x 72.8 cm)

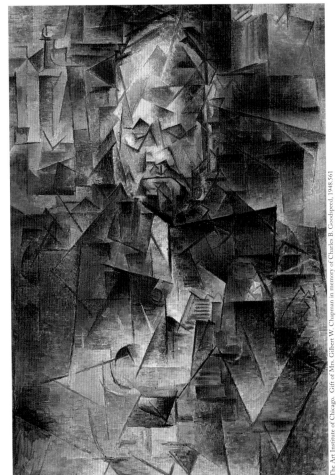

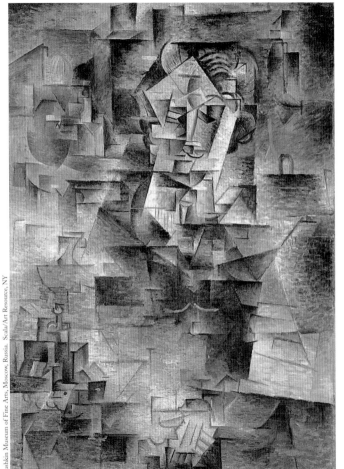

*Portrait of
Ambroise Vollard*
1910
36 ¼ x 25 ⅝"
(92 x 65 cm)

- **Ethereal:** Figures dissolve into shimmering atmospheres.

- **Puzzling:** Caricature-style, each one captures a distinct personality despite radical abstraction (a watch fob, a moustache), with clues emerging bit by bit from the Cubist fragments.

- **Decorative:** The surfaces are beautifully composed rhythms of staccato brushwork and scaffoldlike drawing.

His Cubist portraits move Picasso to the head of the class; other artists begin looking to his example and a full-fledged movement starts to take form. From 1910, the Cubist experiment is more and more manifest in studios and exhibitions throughout Europe. Other experimenters include **Marcel Duchamp** (1887–1968), **Juan Gris** (1887–1927), and **Fernand Léger** (1881–1955).

Cubism's Endless Summer: Céret (1911)

Picasso and Fernande spend the summer of 1911 in the French Pyrénées town of Céret, where they are joined by Braque. The stage is thus set for **one of the most intense collaborations in art history.** It is Braque who makes the big breakthrough (*in a minute*—the suspense won't kill you) and it is Braque who later describes their pioneering efforts as "rather like being roped mountaineers." Working side by side in the same studio that summer, Picasso and Braque encourage and spark each other. Together they scale unexplored new heights.

Sometimes their work is so similar it's difficult to tell whose is whose.

- Both are artists working in the same gray-brown palette and painting still-life subjects.

- Stippled brushwork breaks up the surfaces with nervous energy.

- Sculpture begins to reassert itself: Core volumes pop out of surfaces littered and noisy with pictorial information.

They're moving toward higher and higher degrees of abstraction when suddenly Braque changes the game entirely. Right onto the face of his canvas *The Portuguese,* he stencils text fragments from a poster announcing "Le Grand Bal." Why is this significant? Because:

- **Stenciling** asserts once and for all that *a painting is a flat object,* not a window onto nature or a mirror of reality.

- It also makes possible **a world of co-identities** in which you have an image of a *thing* (say, a newspaper article) in the same frame as the thing itself. It's not a picture of text; it's text slammed right onto the canvas or paper.

We are now accustomed to seeing printed words in art, but back in 1911 it was an unimaginable effrontery to good taste, as shocking as someone slapping a disco poster onto an Impressionist's canvas. *But everything about Cubism was shocking!* The Cubists had broken the mirror that artists were meant to hold up to nature, and held that broken mirror up to the world.

Sound Byte:
"I knew we were painting strange things, but the world seemed a strange place to us."

—PICASSO, on Cubism

Gettin' High

Picasso responds to Braque's innovation *(flash!)* with *Still Life with a Fan*, in which the masthead of the Paris newspaper, *L'Indépendent*, ribbons through the Cubist rubble. Back in Paris, typography from tabloids, advertising, and all manner of printed lettering flows into Picasso's and Braque's canvases. Then Braque ups the ante again, this time with a comb. Having worked as a house painter, Braque is handy with *trompe l'oeil* techniques: By dragging a comb through wet paint, he achieves the look of fake wood grain. Again Picasso follows Braque's lead, going so far as to paint hair on a figure directly with a comb. Both artists are now operating in what is called **High Analytic Cubism:**

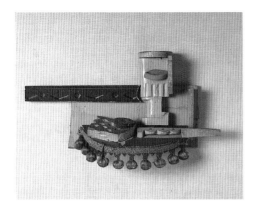

Still Life. 1914
Painted wood
with upholstery
fringe
10 x 18 ⁷/₈ x 4"
(25.5 x 48 x 10 cm)

Tate Gallery, London/
Art Resource, NY

- The world appears pulled apart, intensely analyzed.

- Still lifes are the main motifs.

- The cubes are now transparent fragments that shimmer and hover mysteriously, like flakes of matter held together by a magnetic force.

> **FYI: Talking Pictures**—There's all kinds of punning going on in Picasso's use of text: KUB from a bouillon-cube box stands for *cube;* from *Journal* comes "urnal," a slur of "urinal." On a less giddy note, the rumblings of war and of battles breaking out across Europe are expressed in bits of newspaper text and headlines. Scholars have also pointed out that the Cubists' use of text was a way of literally nourishing what they perceived as the lean vocabulary of traditional painting.

STILL LIFE WITH CHAIR CANING, 1912
Collage of oil, oilcloth, and paper on canvas (oval), surrounded with rope
10 ⁵/₈ x 13 ³/₄" (27 x 35 cm)

What was he thinking? Say you want to pull your viewer into the jazz of modern life—the bustling traffic, the barrage of images reflecting off of cars and windows. How much shattering and shuffling can you get away with and still maintain a sense of reality? And then, what tricks can you throw in?

What's there? Where better to imbibe modern life than at a Paris sidewalk café? This café tabletop is scattered with bits of objects: a pipe, a newspaper, a wine glass. *(Oh! And waiter, I'll have another gin flip...)* It appears to be made of glass, because not only do you see the things on top, but you can also glimpse the caned seat of a café chair below.

Which phase of Cubism? The stripped-down palette of browns and black and white; the indistinct edges and splintered forms of objects scrutinized almost beyond recognition; the confusing *passages* between background and foreground space; the fall of pictorial fragments across the surface that make all parts of the picture equal. What does it spell? **High Analytic Cubism.** The oval format is also typical of this phase: It keeps the eye from wandering into corners (because there aren't any) and creates a more concentrated rapport between viewer and picture.

Bring on the tricks: This painting represents **Picasso's first use of collage.** He uses it to play hard and push the boundaries between art and life. He begins with an old piece of rope, which, as a frame, makes fun of the fancy gilded things that typically surround fine artworks. The rope also works like a lasso, yanking the canvas into the world of materials and things, such as café tabletops with rope edges. Other collage elements are similarly unruly. The caning pattern comes from a strip of decorative oil cloth, which means that a mechanically made picture-of-a-picture is suddenly admitted into an original work of art. A piece of the real world has infiltrated a painting. In short, collage lets Picasso play hard with the conventions that separate art and life, high art and popular culture.

Cool thing to know: The fragment of text ("JOU") from *Le Journal*, the daily newspaper of Paris, is a running gag—a pun on *jeu*, French for "game," and on *jouir*, which means "to enjoy" (with a sexual connotation).

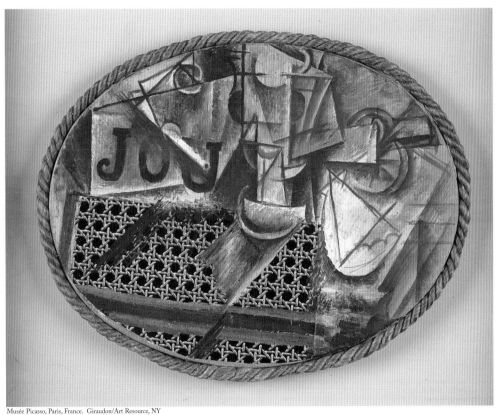

Synthetic Cubism, then Collage

In autumn 1911, Picasso and Fernande break up. That winter he paints *Ma Jolie (Woman with a Zither or Guitar)*, French for "My Pretty One." The words "Ma Jolie" are the title of a popular song and will appear on several new canvases, such as the 1914 *Ma Jolie*. They're also Picasso's term of endearment for his new girlfriend, **Eva Gouel (Marcelle Humbert)**. In 1912, having made room for a little music and joy, the High Analytical phase of Cubism begins to evolve into **Synthetic Cubism.** Color enters the picture (things are getting fanciful and decorative) and subjects become more recognizable. The paintings are more social and, unlike the hermetic studio subjects of before, are full of pop references, puns, the patter of café life, and newspaper clippings. The space is flatter, *passages* are simpler, and edges are more well-defined.

Cubism is carried further in late 1912 by one more innovation from Braque: papier collé, a form of collage using *only* cut paper glued to a drawing or painting ground. Braque makes his first papier collé using decorative paper that he first saw in a shop window in Sorgues, where he and Picasso have just spent another productive Cubist summer. Once again *(flash!)*, Picasso quickly assimilates the new technique into his own art. **The battle has been joined,** he announces to Braque in one of his first papiers collés, by way of a newspaper headline about the Balkan War.

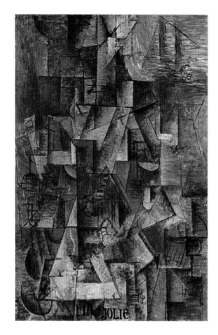

"Ma Jolie"
(Woman with a
Zither or Guitar)
1911–12
39 $^3/_8$ x 25 $^3/_4$"
(100 x 65.4 cm)

The Museum of Modern Art,
New York. Acquired through
the Lillie P. Bliss Bequest.
Photograph © 1999 The Museum
of Modern Art, New York

Collage is considered one of the major innovations of Modern art. In collage, different materials (rope, newspaper, fabric, photographs, glitter, whatever) are synthesized into a new image by pasting them to a paper or canvas ground. (There is also freestanding collage sculpture.) After Cubism, collage becomes an important means of expression for the Dadaists and Surrealists, among others, who are attracted to this technique of editing, slicing, and reassembling the stuff of everyday reality into shocking new images.

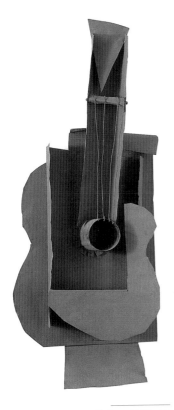

Guitar. 1912–13
Construction of
sheet metal and wire
30 ¹/₂ x 13 ³/₄
x 7 ⁵/₈"
(77.5 x 35 x 19.3 cm)
The Museum of Modern Art,
New York. Gift of the artist.
Photograph © 1999 The Museum
of Modern Art, New York

Cubist Sculpture: "I call it a guitar"

The dead end that Picasso had run up against in 1909, trying (via the bronze head of Fernande) to give sculptural form to Cubism, is bypassed in 1912 when he approaches the problem from an entirely new avenue. After seeing some paper constructions by Braque, he *(flash!)* makes a *Guitar* (1912–13) out of sheet metal with wire for the strings. These are metal-worker's, not artist's, materials. And compared to traditional sculpture, this thing is totally whacky. When a perplexed viewer asked Picasso, "What is it— a sculpture, a collage, a toy, a piece of junk?" Picasso said, "I call it a guitar." It laid the foundation for a new approach to sculpture: *no modeling, no carving, just assembling.*

The End of an Affair

The lovers spend the spring of 1913 in Céret, where Picasso works on more papiers collés, returning briefly to Barcelona for the funeral of his father. Upon their return to Paris in the fall, he paints *Woman in an Armchair,* a curious work that merges the colors of Analytic Cubism with the patterns of Synthetic Cubism.

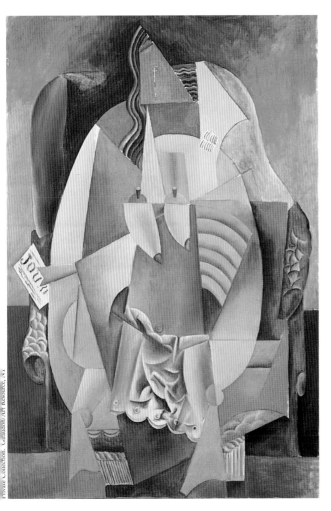

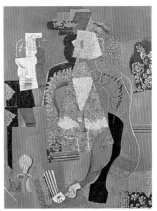

ABOVE
Portrait of a Young Girl. 1914
51 ¹/₄ x 38 ¹/₈"
(130 x 97 cm)

LEFT
Woman in an Armchair. 1913
Oil and encaustic on canvas
51 ¹/₄ x 35"
(130.2 x 88.8 cm)

On August 2, 1914, war is declared between France and Germany. As a Spaniard, Picasso is not drafted into service, but his friends are. Braque returns from the front wounded in 1916 and later continues to develop a synthetic style of painting. Apollinaire is wounded in the head, then dies of the flu in November 1918, just days before the Armistice. On December 14, 1915, Eva dies of tuberculosis. In many respects, **Picasso is now left completely alone;** the years of collaboration and critical community that surrounded Cubism are over.

Beyond the Beyond

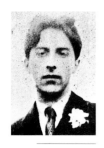

Jean Cocteau
1917

Where to go from here? Alone, Picasso continues to push the **decorative potential of Synthetic Cubism** into a rococo imagery of Pointillist polka dots, harlequin checks, brilliant colors, and other decorative devices. In late 1915, he meets the poet and playwright **Jean Cocteau** (1889–1963), who introduces him to the worlds of ballet and theater. After moving to the outskirts of Paris in early summer 1916, Picasso agrees to work on a commission offered by the dance impresario **Sergei Diaghilev** (1872–1929) to design the costumes and décor for a new ballet, the avant-garde production of *Parade.* The scenario, by Cocteau, involves a group of actors—including a Chinese conjurer and an acrobat—who ply their talents outside a theater to entice spectators into the house. Although the 1917 Paris debut is a disaster—the audience is scandalized by **Erik Satie**'s (1866–1925) music of typewriters and sirens, which are too close to the current wartime acoustic landscape for comfort—it initiates a series of collaborations between Picasso and the theater. It is also the occasion for him to meet his new lover, the ballerina **Olga Kholkhlova,** one of the dancers in the troupe, whose beauty he captures in *Portrait of Olga on an Armchair.* He marries her on July 12, 1918.

Meanwhile, Picasso's international reputation and financial circumstances increase exponentially from year to year. By the 1920s, he has practically become the legend we know. And he's only in his 40s, with 50 years to go! But where do you go from Cubism? We know that Picasso is not the kind of guy to stick to one routine, nor will he plod along, slowly evolving new styles. Let's face it: He has full command of all the pictorial languages a Modern artist could desire. He can create images (painted, drawn, sculpted) as a traditional realist, as an expressionist, or as an avant-garde abstract artist. Picasso's talent could easily fuel 20 careers. And in a way it does, but all in one artist's work. **Picasso spends the rest of his career working simultaneously in a virtuoso variety of modes of representation.** Any given image is as apt to be:

- As classically ordered as it is baroquely twisted.

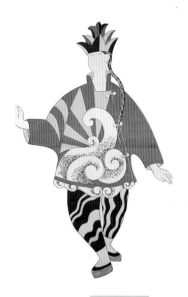

Chinese costume from *Parade* 1917

Giraudon/Art Resource, NY

79

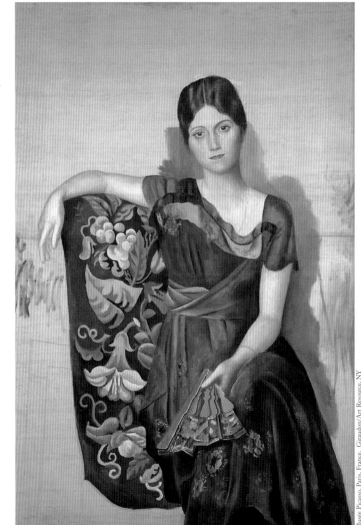

- As realistically representational as it is conceptually abstract.

- As sculpturally monumental as it is expressively graphic.

From Invention to Metamorphosis

From 1914 forward, it's the act of **transformation** that increasingly engages his interest. Think of Picasso's post-Cubism art as a self-sustaining system that continuously reinvents itself in terms of *itself.* Not to say there aren't any more *flashes!* of inspiration from the outside world, or new problems, or thematic developments. But with so many languages in place, his art doesn't respond in a singular or linear way of thinking. Nonetheless, **Picasso's post-Cubism art boils down to relatively few essentials.** The first is that there is much to see: Picasso is active, prolific, and makes powerful pictures to the end. Having created a strong repertoire of styles and invented a valid conceptual approach through Cubism, he is now free to become completely absorbed in his own art.

This is when **the really fascinating pictorial thinking begins.** Simply by tweaking the colors and rearranging the forms, he can change an image of a woman from a stark and repulsive **nightmare** (*Figures by the Sea*, 1931, on page 90) to an image of lush and inviting serenity (*Seated Woman with a Book*, 1932, on page 94). It is remarkable how fluidly Picasso moves from one pictorial language to another.

THREE MUSICIANS, 1921
80 ¹/₂ x 74 ¹/₈" (203 x 188 cm)
Philadelphia Museum of Art: A. E. Gallatin Collection

What was he thinking? About the decorative and theatrical possibilities of Cubism.

Who are they? Each of the three musicians seated at the table represents a stock character of the Italian commedia dell'arte: the Harlequin (in the checks), Pulcinella (in the black mask and white costume), and a Friar (in burlap).

What kind of Cubism? *Three Musicians* is considered the culmination of Picasso's Synthetic Cubist style. He's pushed the flatness of the imagery and decorative arrangement of colors and patterns to an extreme. Indeed, the elements of this composition appear locked into place like pieces in a jigsaw puzzle.

Very theatrical: At the time this picture is made, Picasso is intensely involved in a series of theatrical collaborations. In 1920, he designs boldly Cubist sets and costumes for *Pulcinella*, a ballet with music by Igor Stravinsky. The style and imagery of *Three Musicians* show him thinking about translating his stage experience to a painting on canvas.

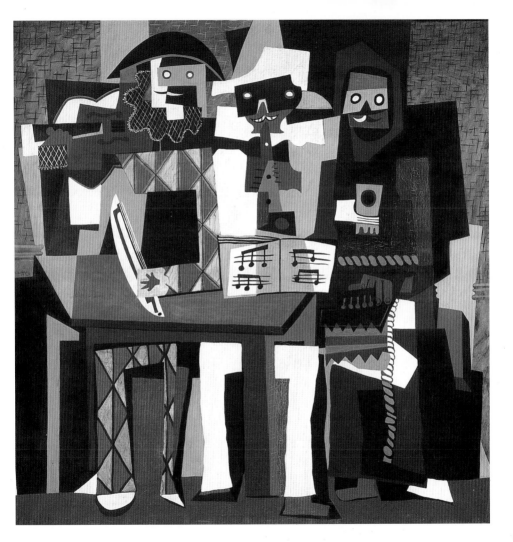

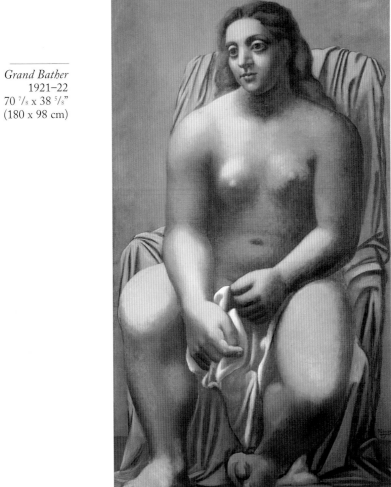

Grand Bather
1921–22
70 ⁷/₈ x 38 ⁵/₈"
(180 x 98 cm)

Daily Life after Cubism

The more famous Picasso gets, the more isolated he strives to become, withdrawing into the hermetic world of his own images and their creation. Neither the First nor the Second World War pose much distraction. Basically, Picasso keeps to a daily work schedule, living in Paris and vacationing in the South of France, often with a complicated ménage of women and children in tow. (In one farcical episode in 1939, he takes two mistresses, one with a baby, on the same holiday, intending that they not find out about each another. They do.)

Picasso's Neoclassicism: The 1920s

During the early 1920s, *the cool classicism* of **Jean-Auguste-Dominique Ingres** (1780–1867) and a *colossal sense of scale* intersect in Picasso's art to produce an idiosyncratic **Neoclassical style** based on the human figure. This work has been seen by historians as representative of a postwar call to order. Indeed, it does look like **an antidote to the non-perspective systems of Primitivism and fragmented reality of Cubism** with which Picasso had been involved in the years up to and throughout the war. Nonetheless, nothing is sacred: Picasso's classic subjects prove to be equal targets for analysis and re-tooling. In his *Grand Bather*, a female model poses with classical drapery, exuding an attitude of calm solidity, *but her feet are at least 30 sizes too large!* These distortions may be more elegantly drawn into the whole, but they are no less radical. It's not long before Neoclassicism is dropped into Picasso's vast kit of pictorial styles along with all the others it has seemingly opposed.

Sculpting in the Stables: Boisgeloup

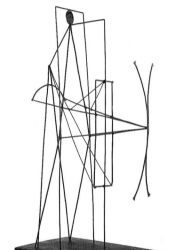

Sculpture continues to be an important area of invention for Picasso throughout the rest of his career. Deploying a variety of techniques, he sculpts plaster and clay models and **assembles found objects** that are cast into bronze. In 1928, his friend, the Spanish sculptor **Julio González** (1876–1942) teaches him to weld. Picasso immediately creates **a series of wire constructions** that he sees as drawings in space. In turn, they inform his paintings with a tensile new structure and (for lack of a better word) *wiry* form of abstraction. In 1931, he purchases a 17th-century manor house in Boisgeloup, on the outskirts of Paris, and transforms its stables into a sculpture and printmaking studio. Among the works produced there are a series of sculptural heads of a young woman and a series of 57 etchings (called the **Vollard Suite,** after the dealer who published them), starring **Marie-Thérèse Walter,** Picasso's secret mistress and muse since 1927.

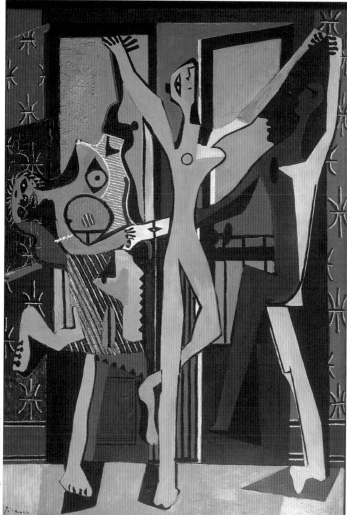

LEFT
The Three Dancers
1925
84 ⁵/₈ x 55 ⁷/₈" (215
x 142 cm)

OPPOSITE
Wire Construction
(offered as a model
for a monument
to Guillaume
Apollinaire). 1928
Metal wire
23 ⁷/₈ x 13 x 5 ⁷/₈"
(60.5 x 33 x 15 cm)

A predominant movement in art during the 1930s and 40s. It originated in French literature, claiming special ties to Symbolist poetry of the late 19th century. According to André Breton, one of its leading spokespersons, the movement attempted to reconcile the worlds of the dream and everyday reality in "a sort of absolute reality," or "surreality." (*Sur* is French for "above.") Deeply influenced by **Sigmund Freud's** (1856–1939) theories of psychoanalysis, the Surrealists sought the irrational and complex over the composed and absolute. One of their most significant contributions to Modernism was the technique of *automatism*, by which the artist attempts to draw (or write) without stopping to think, as if tapping directly into the unconscious mind.

Picasso and Surrealism: The 1930s

Recognized as a cultural authority figure, Picasso no longer runs with the pack, but leads from a distance. New movements claim to adopt him—most significantly, Surrealism. In January 1925, several pages from one of Picasso's sketchbooks are published in the Surrealist journal, *La Révolution surréaliste.* The drawings—abstract constellations of dots connected by lines bristling with energy—demonstrate what it is that the Surrealists love about Picasso: the seeming *automatism* of his art. (They're also big into Picassso's Primitivism, since they too are fascinated by the seeming magic and fetishistic powers of tribal art.)

In July, *Les Demoiselles d'Avignon* is reproduced for the first time ever in the same magazine with a statement from the editor, **André Breton** (1896–1966), announcing: "We claim him as one of ours." Picasso returns their interest *(flash!)* by producing works throughout the 1930s that are considered Surrealist. (He even scribbles some Surrealist poems and a play.)

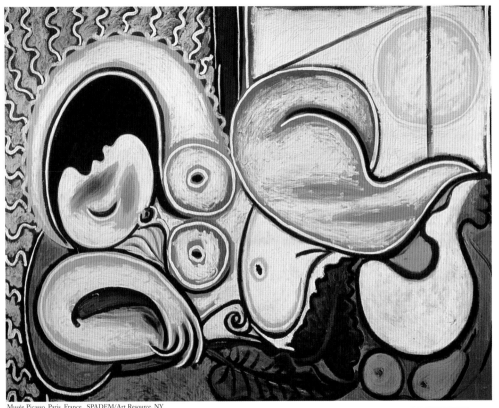

Sleeping Nude
1932
51 $\frac{1}{4}$ x 63 $\frac{3}{8}$"
(130 x 161.7 cm)

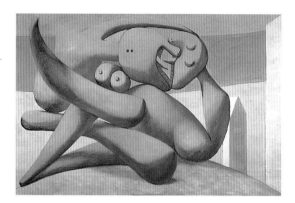

Figures by the Sea
1931. 51 $^{3}/_{8}$ x 77"
(130.5 x 195.5 cm)

Musée Picasso, Paris, France.
Giraudon/Art Resource, NY

Surrealism in Picasso's Art

Once you start to examine it, the relationship between Picasso and Surrealism actually runs pretty deep throughout his work of the 1930s. But you can get the essential gist in a couple of images. (Recall: The Surrealists were into Freud, who had a lot to say about human sexuality, not much of it attractive).

1. *Figures by the Sea* (1931): The way the figures appear to have been metamorphosed into a horrid pair of carnal and cannibalizing insects: that's Surrealism.

2. *Weeping Woman* (1937): The way the lurid colors, spiky forms, and cruel caricature all create a psychic expression of a needy and dangerous lady: that's Surrealism.

Weeping Woman
1937
23 $^5/_8$ x 19 $^1/_4$"
(60 x 49 cm)

THE DREAM, 1932

51 ¹/₄ x 38 ¹/₈" (130 x 97 cm)

Private Collection. Giraudon/Art Resource, NY

What was he thinking? About voluptuousness!

How: Every line and color—to say nothing of the model who is so deeply sunk into reverie that she doesn't notice her blouse is slipping off—serves the voluptuousness of this image.

Colossal feeling: See those sensual contours? It's the same line Picasso used in his Neoclassical images, but here the image isn't cold and remote. Quite the opposite: The colors are dazzlingly fresh and there's a strong decorative appeal that comes straight out of Synthetic Cubism.

To sleep, perchance to dream: A pink shadow falls across the woman's face, dividing it into a full moon under eclipse. She embodies the dream state as explicitly as any Surrealist muse.

Caress and nourish: In her passive state, she is also a tantalizing invitation to ravishment and pleasure. The lines of the picture caress her and she caresses herself. One armrest is a succulent peach. One breast bobs into view. *If this isn't pictorial seduction replete with the promise of fulfillment, what is?*

Cool thing to know: The model is Marie-Thérèse Walter. Her imagery is practically a landscape that Picasso explores in painting and sculpture throughout the 1930s.

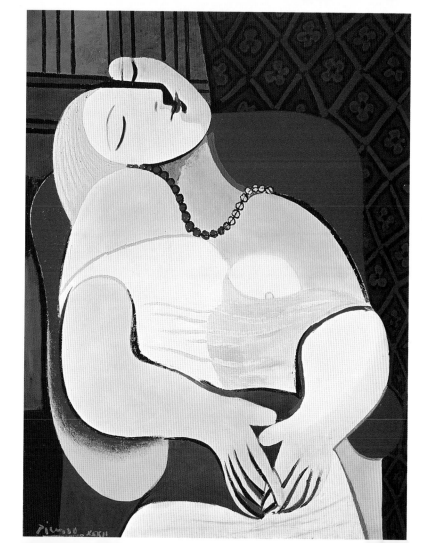

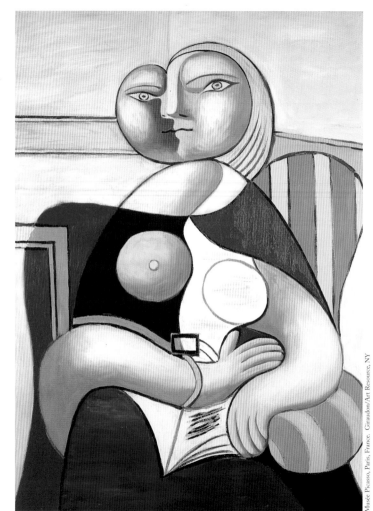

Seated Woman with a Book. 1932
51 ¼ x 38 ⅛"
(130 x 97 cm)

War Paths

By 1935, Picasso's marriage to Olga is kaput; her grand airs and lofty social ambitions are too much for him. After she discovers that her husband's mistress of the past eight years is pregnant, Olga takes their 14-year old son, Paulo, on the annual beach holiday without his father. Her refusal to grant Picasso a divorce casts the artist into a **period of isolation and depression,** which he calls "the worst time of my life." Picasso invites his old friend from Spain, Jaime Sabartés, to move in. Sabartés assumes the role of Picasso's secretary and confidante (and will become an essential fixture of the artist's life until Sabartés's death in 1968). **Maïa,** Picasso's daughter with Marie-Thérèse, is born that October. Under the name "Ruiz," the love family hides out together during spring 1936 in Juan-les-Pins, where Picasso works on a series of Minotaur images.

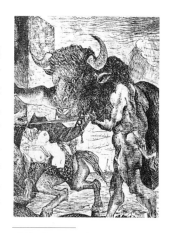

Minotauromachy
1935. Etching and scraper
19 ⁵/₈ x 27 ¹/₄"
(49.8 x 69.3 cm)
Musée Picasso, Paris, France

FYI: Minotaurs—The 1/2 man, 1/2 bull is a recurrent image in Picasso's work that he begins to explore in 1928. In 1933, he designs the cover for the first issue of a Surrealist magazine called *Minotaur*. In 1935, he introduces the strange hybrid **Minotauromachy** (bullfights with Minotaurs), often with a female toreador who is brutally and sexually mauled by her beastly opponent.

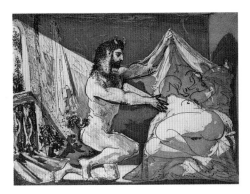

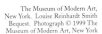

Faun Unveiling a Sleeping Woman 1936. Sugar lift aquatint and scraper, printed in black, plate 12 ¹/₂ x 16 ⁷/₈." (31.7 x 41.7 cm)

The Museum of Modern Art, New York. Louise Reinhardt Smith Bequest. Photograph © 1999 The Museum of Modern Art, New York

Picasso learns of the **outbreak of the Spanish Civil War** when he returns to Paris in July 1936. In August, hanging out on the Riviera with some Surrealists, he becomes involved with the artist **Dora Maar,** who happens to speak fluent Spanish. She helps him find a huge new studio in Paris, located on the rue des Grands-Augustins, where, in 1937, he creates his grandiose **antifascist statement:** the 27-foot long mural entitled *Guernica.*

Dora Maar photographs the progressive stages of *Guernica* as Picasso works on it. Over the next few years, she continues to see Picasso as he also sees Marie-Thérèse. Picasso paints them both, sometimes in an identical pose. In 1938, he introduces the theme of cocks (the poultry version of a bull) to his repertoire, all the while trying (not always successfully) to keep the two women from knowing about each other.

*Portrait of
Marie–Thérèse*
1937
39 $^3/_8$ x 31 $^7/_8$"
(100 x 81 cm)

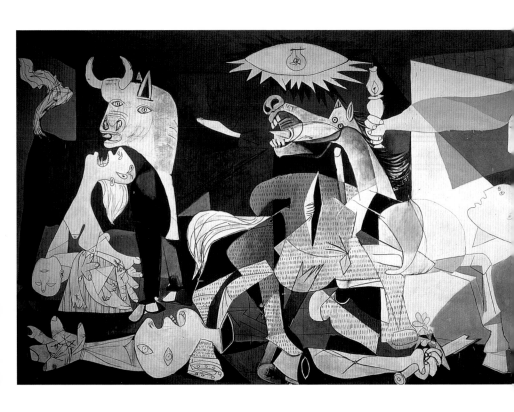

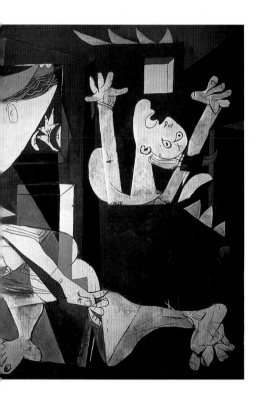

GUERNICA, 1937

11'5 ½" x 25'5 ¾" (349.3 x 776.6 cm)

Museo Nacional Centro de Arte Reina Sofia, Madrid, Spain.
Giraudon/Art Resource, NY

What was he thinking? He wishes to paint a tragedy on the horrors of war (hello, Goya!).

What is it? A mural commission. In January 1937, Picasso is invited by the Spanish Republican Government to create a mural for the Spanish Pavilion at the World's Fair in Paris that will open in June.

Background: The Spanish Civil War breaks out on July 18, 1937 between the populist Spanish Republicans and the fascists under General Francisco Franco. By January of that year, Picasso—a Spaniard with strong populist sympathies—has already started a suite of satiric etchings and written a poem against Franco. These images eventually segue into those of the mural: "...cries of children cries of women cries of birds cries of flowers cries of timbers and of stones...cries of furniture of beds of chairs of curtains of pots of cats of papers cries of odors "(from Picasso's 1937 etching "Dream and Lie of Franco").

A terrible flash! Picasso is still casting around for a theme when terrible news reaches Paris. On April 26, German planes under Franco's orders bomb the Basque village of Guernica, attacking in midday when people are out and about in the streets. The massacre's aftermath is documented in stories and photographs in the Paris newspaper, *Ce Soir*. This becomes the imagery of Picasso's mural.

An abstraction: Picasso represents the specific event through a grand allegorical image. It evolves from the conflation of existing works, such as the cartoonlike etchings for the "Dream and Lie of Franco" and the fantastically violent scenes of his *Minotauromachy* series. He makes over 50 preparatory sketches in the process.

Screams tragedy: Abstracted into somber tones of gray, charcoal, and black and white, *Guernica* is a painting of graphic intensity. Every inch of it *shrieks*—the screaming mouths of every man, woman, child, horse, bull, and cock; the clenched gestures, spiked forms, painful distortions. It is richly theatrical in its use of shallow cutout forms, proscenium space, and actors who sweep across a stage, gesturing dramatically. In terms of Picasso's art, *Guernica* is very much *"Les Demoiselles d'Avignon* meets *Parade."*

Postscript: Picasso goes on to create two more major antiwar paintings in his lifetime; both are painted in grisaille and strike the same high-pitched emotional tenor of dramatic outrage. Drafted as a compendium to *Guernica*, his painting *Charnal House* (1944–45) commemorates the victims of the Jewish Holocaust; the image was informed in its final stages by photographs taken after the liberation of the concentration camp at Dachau. And *Massacre in Korea* (1951) is Picasso's pictorial protest against American intervention in Korea.

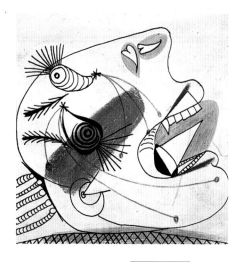

A study for *Guernica*

Wartime

Shortly after war is declared in September 1939, Picasso finds himself in an embarrassing situation when his two mistresses discover that he's brought them both on holiday. He returns to Paris, where all three fall back into their routine deceptions and Picasso adjusts to life under the German Occupation. He resourcefully turns the bathroom of his apartment on the rue des Grands-Augustins into a sculpture studio and is photographed for *Life* Magazine, hanging out in cafés to keep warm. When the Germans offer to provide the famous artist with extra fuel, Picasso defiantly turns down their favors with the much-quoted quip: "A Spaniard is never cold." However, like Matisse, **Picasso spends the war years living in relative luxury,** remaining productive in his studio and having his work represented in exhibitions

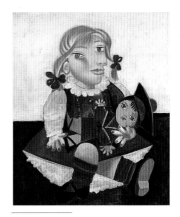

Maïa with a Doll
1938. 28 ³/₄ x 23 ⁵/₈"
(73 x 60 cm)

Musée Picasso, Paris, France.
Giraudon/Art Resource, NY

around the world. Both artists are considered national heroes for staying in France when they could easily have fled. (Picasso turns down an invitation of exile to America.)

OPPOSITE
*Picasso at home
with canvases,
tribal artifacts,
and bric-a-brac*

Postwar Picasso: Communism and Ceramics

Paris is liberated from the German Occupation in August 1944. In October, Picasso's work is the subject of a **special exhibition at the Salon d'Automne in Paris.** It's a big deal, because (absolutely unlike Matisse) Picasso has never participated in the French public system of annual exhibitions of contemporary art. Plus, it's an opportunity to exclaim his new sense of allegiance, not only to France, but to the **Communist Party,** which he has just joined.

Sound Byte:

"Until the day when Spain can welcome me back, the French Communist Party [has] opened its arms to me and I found in it those that I most value, the greatest scientists, the greatest poets, all those beautiful faces of Parisian insurgents...[and] I am once more among my brothers."

—PICASSO, proclaiming his faith in Communism, October 1944

Public outcry from conservatives on the Right is met with rejoicing from intellectuals on the Left, including the Existentialist philosopher

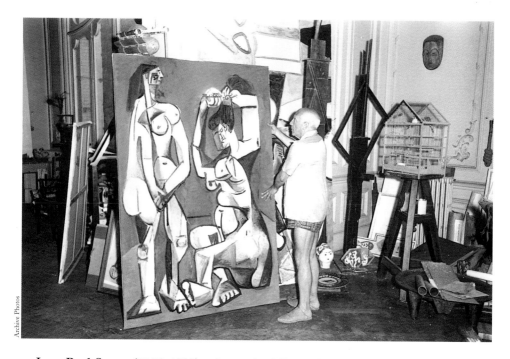

Archive Photos

Jean-Paul Sartre (1905–1980), who applaud Picasso's conversion to Communism. After the din dies down, Picasso returns to his regimen of studio work, but with a new mistress on the scene. Although Picasso met the young art student **Françoise Gilot** in 1943, they don't become intimately involved until 1945. That November he also discovers and **becomes fascinated with the technique of lithography** because it allows him to document the metamorphosis of a single image. From

December 1945 to January 1946, he works on a series of lithographs of a bull that begins realistically enough but that—11 prints later—ends up as a few representative lines. Voilà! Reduction of bull. In 1946, while Picasso and Françoise are staying in Ménerbes, he is intrigued by the owls that encircle the village every evening. (Also fascinating is the fact that they're staying in a house that Picasso bought for Dora, where he receives almost daily correspondence from Marie-Thérèse.) The **imagery of owls** enters the work the following year, when Picasso also takes up ceramics.

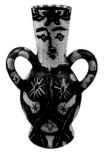

Anthropomorphous vase. c. 1960

> **FYI: Ceramics**—In 1947 Picasso starts making ceramics *like mad.* In the summer of 1936, he and Dora Maar had discovered the French village of Vallauris, on the French Riviera, where pottery had been produced since Roman times. When he returns in 1947, Picasso energizes what has become a slumping trade by creating at the workshop over 2,000 ceramics in just one year. *(Quick calculation: That's at least five objects a day with no rest on Sundays.)* As explicitly decorative objects, Picasso's ceramics are often quite playful and whimsical. One of the treats in visiting the Musée Picasso in Paris is encountering examples of them perched in corners and over doorways throughout the galleries.

Bird Man of Vallauris (1947–55)

After the 1947 birth of their son **Claude,** Picasso and Françoise move into villa La Galloise above the town of Vallauris, where Picasso singlehandedly revitalizes the centuries-old ceramics trade with his furious production there. As a famous artist, chic Communist, and international figure, Picasso's presence and endorsement are increasingly in demand. His lithographic image, the *Dove of Peace*, becomes the emblem of an international Peace Congress held in 1949. It also provides the namesake for Picasso's daughter **Paloma** (Spanish for "dove"), born the same year. Less than three years later, Picasso's relationship with Françoise is on the wane. It ends officially after he meets **Jacqueline Roque** in 1953, when he embarks on an extended series of drawings on the theme of the painter and his model. Throughout the 1950s, he engages in **studies of favorite old masters**—most remarkably, the **40 variations he makes after Velázquez's *Las Meninas*.**

Women of Algiers, or Picasso and Matisse

In 1954, Henri Matisse dies. As Picasso's great opposite, Matisse is 12 years older, but they are exact artistic peers. Throughout the first half of the 20th century, their careers are so parallel that if you hold their résumés side-by-side, you can almost match their respective achievements and breakthroughs: Matisse deals with issues of color, Picasso with issues of form, and so on. Aware of each other as such, they are the two dons of Modernist abstraction, working at a distance, but always keeping an eye on each other. To describe their vast temperamental differences, Picasso, the bad boy, likes to say that he is the

OVERLEAF

TOP LEFT
Diego Velázquez,
Las Meninas (The Maids of Honor)
1656. 10'5" x 9'
(320 x 270 cm)

BOTTOM LEFT
Las Meninas #1, after Velázquez
1957
76 ³/₈ x 102 ³/₈"
(194 x 260 cm)

RIGHT
Las Meninas #14, after Velázquez
1957
18 ¹/₄" x 12'4"
(46 x 375 cm)

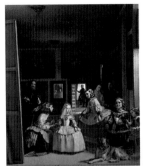

Museo del Prado, Madrid

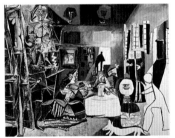

Museo Picasso, Barcelona, Spain. Giraudon/Art Resource, NY

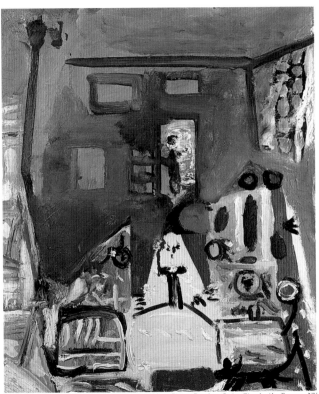

Museo Picasso, Barcelona, Spain. Giraudon/Art Resource, NY

South Pole, while he deems Matisse, the bourgeois elder statesman, the North Pole. Matisse was known to idolize the artist **Eugène Delacroix** (1798–1863), whose influential theories on color and travels inspired Matisse's own trips to North Africa and the harem themes in his art. So when Picasso embarks on a series of **variations on Delacroix's** *The Women of Algiers* in 1955, the year after Matisse's death, how can it not signify a tribute to his dead rival?

Sound Byte:

> *"All things considered, there's only Matisse."*

> —PICASSO

Finding the Mask: The Last Paintings (1955–73)

In 1955, **Picasso settles in the South of France,** first at the villa La Californie, overlooking Cannes; then, in 1958, at the 14th-century Château de Vauvenargues, set in the same Provençal landscape near Aix-en-Provence that Cézanne made famous in his paintings; and finally, in 1961, in his new villa, Notre-Dame-de-Vie, in the hills above Cannes, near the village of Mougins. Picasso devotes his final years (all 18 of them) to graphic works of great delicacy and to expressive canvases, painted with crude urgency. Almost without exception, the subject is **the figure**—usually an allegorical character,

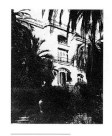

La Californie
c. 1955

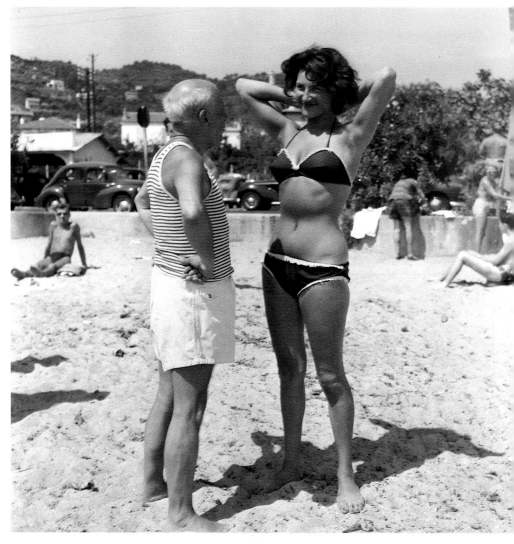

dwarf or a virgin, who is often agape (i.e., mouth wide open) and who bristles with exposed sexual parts, which leads some to interpret them as Picasso's defiant ravings against his own sexual waning and imminent death. In his later years, Picasso himself says he is obsessed with one project: **"I must absolutely find the mask."** Many of these paintings look back with staring eyes and totemlike visages, expressing perhaps a faint echo of what Picasso experienced years earlier when he found himself alone at the Trocadéro museum in the revelatory presence of African sculpture. **Picasso dies at Mougins on April 8, 1973** at the age of 91 and is buried on the grounds of the Château de Vauvenargues.

Picasso's Greatness: The Big Seduction

Like all Modernists, Picasso devoted his life to searching for **new forms of representation** based on issues of abstraction. He worked with an **erotic energy** to dominate, through art, virtually everything that fell subject to his vision—women, in particular. For contemporary viewers, Picasso's machismo is as legendary as his apparent misogyny is troublesome. What to make of a depiction of his mistress, the artist Dora Maar, that transforms her (the ambitious woman) into a weeping Gorgon? Or his images of the

OPPOSITE
On the beach at Vallauris

BELOW
Goat. 1950
Bronze (after assemblage of palm leaf, ceramic flower-pots, wicker basket, metal elements, and plaster)
46 ³/₈ x 56 ³/₈ x 27 ³/₄"
(117.7 x 143.1 x 70.5 cm)

Musée Picasso, Paris, France.
Giraudon/Art Resource, NY

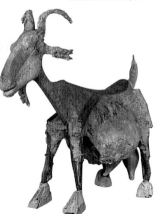

buxom young blond, Marie-Thérèse Walter, as a delectable sex object? More than portraits of particular individuals, Picasso's **images of women** appear as expressions of his own appetites, anxieties, and imaginative power. And these expressions spill overwhelmingly into every image he made. No matter if it's a picture of a woman, a bull, or a flower—what you see first and foremost is Picasso and his **creative intensity.**

Sound Byte:

"Indeed, Picasso is the very model of the inflationary artist, not simply because prices for his work seem to be on a dizzying spiral ever upward, but because as the great prestidigitator, the wizard who turns debris around him—newspaper, withered leaves, bicycle parts—to creative account, he has been raised to the level of a Midas whose every touch is golden."

—ROSALIND E. KRAUSS, art historian,
in *The Picasso Papers,* 1998

When you look at a work by Picasso, you are drawn into a visual experience founded on the act of creating a picture: You see him thinking about *making it* and when you see another Picasso, you see him thinking about *making it all over again.* The pressure to perform, attended by corollary fears of failure or, worse, impotence, never dwindled but built explosively throughout his art into an overpowering force. Completely **driven by his desire to make art,** Picasso approached every picture as a

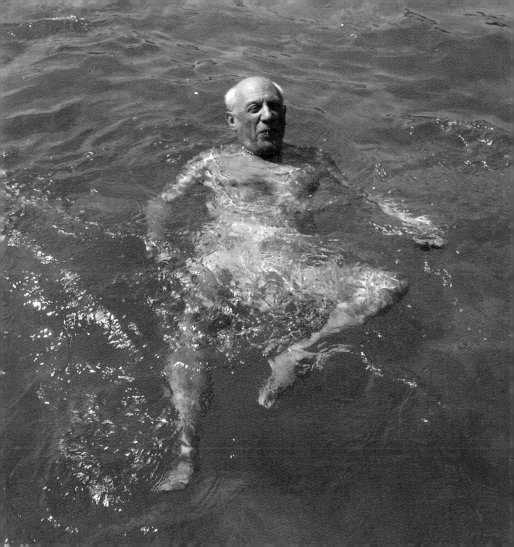

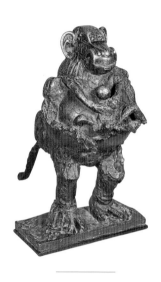

possibility to **formulate anew** one of the essential questions of Modern art: What **makes** this picture? He made the answer as engaging and apparent as *It's me looking at those caressing lines and sensual colors and seeing the figure of a woman transformed into a powerful image of pure pictorial seduction.* He became, in a sense, his own movement—**a Minotaur figure of Modern art** whose pictures clearly and continuously re-think themselves. Therein rests the greatness of Pablo Picasso.

Baboon and Young
1951. After
original plaster
with metal, ceramic
elements, and
two toy cars)
21 x 13 ¹/₄ x 20 ³/₄"
(53.3 x 33.7 x 52.7 cm)